INHABITED WORLD
New & Selected Poems
1970–1995

Also by John Allman

POETRY
Walking Four Ways in the Wind
(Princeton University Press, 1979)

Clio's Children
(New Directions, 1985)

Scenarios for a Mixed Landscape
(New Directions, 1986)

Curve Away from Stillness: Science Poems
(New Directions, 1989)

FICTION
Descending Fire & Other Stories
(New Directions, 1994)

INHABITED WORLD
New & Selected Poems
1970–1995

John Allman

The Wallace Stevens Society Press
Potsdam, NY 13699

© 1985, 1986, 1987, 1988, 1989, 1990, 1991, 1995 by John Allman
All rights reserved
Manufactured in the United States of America

The poems in New Poems were first published in *The Antioch Review* ("Refigurations"), *Memphis State Review* ("Five Cats and a Discussion of the Soul, After a Trip to South Carolina"), *Pacific Review* ("Emma's Loss of Hearing"), *Poetry Northwest* ("Taking the 9:26 Out of Katonah," "A House," "Reading the *Times* in the Car Wash"), *The Quarterly* ("On the Blackness of Sidney," "On the Extraction of Eileen's Wisdom Tooth," "The Expulsion," "Thinking of Gustav Klimt, with Molly on My Lap," "*Les Amoureux en Vert*," "Waving to Mr. Romney"). The poems from *Walking Four Ways in the Wind*, © 1979 by Princeton University Press, are here reprinted by permission of Princeton University Press. The rights to the following collections by John Allman are held by New Directions Publishing Corporation, 80 Eighth Avenue, New York, N.Y. 10011, to whom any permissions requests should be addressed. Poems are here reprinted from the collections by permission of New Directions: *Clio's Children*, © 1985 by John Allman; *Scenarios for a Mixed Landscape*, © 1986 by John Allman; *Curve Away from Stillness*, © 1989 by John Allman.

Library of Congress Cataloging-in-Publication Data

Allman, John, 1935–
  Inhabited world : new & selected poems 1970–1995 / John Allman.
      p.   cm.
  ISBN 0-9648056-0-X (pbk. : alk. paper)
  I. Title.
PS3551.L46I54   1995
811'.54—dc20   95-25075
                                                                                  CIP

Poetry Series Editor
John N. Serio

The Wallace Stevens Society Press
Box 5750 Clarkson University
Potsdam, NY 13699

this book in all its seasons is for Eileen

CONTENTS

Preface	9
New Poems (1995)	13
Taking the 9:26 Out of Katonah	15
Emma's Loss of Hearing	17
On the Blackness of Sidney	18
A House	20
On the Extraction of Eileen's Wisdom Tooth	21
The Expulsion	22
Refigurations	24
Thinking of Gustav Klimt, with Molly on My Lap	26
Five Cats and a Discussion of the Soul,	
After a Trip to South Carolina	28
Reading the *Times* in the Car Wash	30
Les Amoureux en Vert	32
Waving to Mr. Romney	34
from *Curve Away from Stillness* (1989)	37
Chemistry	39
Biology	62
from *Scenarios for a Mixed Landscape* (1986)	73
Legend of the Miniature Rose	75
Buying a Gift for Liesl in Bloomingdale's	76
Flower	77
Southern Exposure	78
Variation on Heat and Silence	79
The Birth of Time	80
The Scattering	81
Winter Solstice	82
Scenarios for a Mixed Landscape	83
On Ellsworth Kelly's Sculptures	86
The Window	87
The Material Conversions	88

The Dog	89
Running	90
Eclipse	91
Disincarnating	92
Glen Island	93
Clouds	94
Hearing Noises	96
The Token	97
World Without You	98

from *Clio's Children* (1985) — 101

Dostoevsky at Semyonov Square, 1849	103
George Sand at Palaiseau, 1865	107
William Morris Boating up the Thames to Kelmscott Manor, 1880	111
Emma Goldman Deported to Russia, 1919	116
Bruno Bettelheim at Dachau, 1938	121
Eugene O'Neill at Tao House, 1941	124

from *Walking Four Ways in the Wind* (1979) — 127

Creedmoor: The Locked Ward	129
The Knuckler	132
Widow	134
Siblings	135
Release	136
The Soul Plays You Bet Your Life	142
The Soul Grown Lazy	144
The Soul Walks Out	145
Surgery	146
A Former Life	147
Nana's Visit	148
Reconciliation	149
Personal	150
The Weeper	151

Notes — 153

Preface

In arranging these poems in reverse chronological order, I imagine that reading them is like looking at a tree from its uppermost leaves down to the splay of trunk where tree meets earth, and the hint of roots beneath. There is something interesting about going through a progression downwards and backwards. But the poems of twenty-five years ago seemed to me at the time I wrote them complete in themselves and part of nothing else, and I am loath to claim for the poems that are the top of the tree a higher life and more complexity than those at the base possess. On the other hand, to arrange the poems with the earliest first, I'm afraid that the lesser-to-greater fallacy is even harder to avoid. The problem is how to talk about the differences between the old and the new. I would not these days write unpunctuated poems. I thought I had abandoned that style in the 1970s. Yet in the mid-1980s, after working with the speculative lyric, and taking on the task of the science poems in *Curve Away from Stillness,* I found that only an unpunctuated style fit my needs.

Were I to talk of a developed life, in another sense, I'd say that the poems from the first book, *Walking Four Ways in the Wind,* are deeply enmeshed in family matters, showing a mind and a life trying to break free. But the poems from *Clio's Children* suggest that what appeared to be personal and familial might have had its origin in something historical. I am only just beginning to understand why I went to history poems after the kind of personal book that *Walking Four Ways in the Wind* was. I thought I was shifting into something other than autobiography. For the six years I worked on *Clio's Children,* I found myself caught in a different kind of continuum, where the cultural-political, the artistic, the individual life were crisscrossing ripples in one stream, and I learned just how complex survival is. A liberation of sorts does, I think, show in the poems from *Scenarios for a Mixed Landscape* and *Curve Away from Stillness.* The speaker in those poems leaps into nature, art, science—love—and brings with him a past no longer so trammeling.

I dare not say much about the New Poems except to note that I had tried after the speculative/narrative forms of *Curve Away from Stillness* to settle into more quotidian contexts, something more obviously social, while still being drawn to the meditative, transformative power of art works. In any case, throughout this entire process of writing poems and, now, organizing them, I have tried to show that we are implicated in something very large as often as something very small.

Katonah, N.Y.
July 27, 1995

New Poems (1995)

TAKING THE 9:26 OUT OF KATONAH

thinking of Steven

Off-peak time. Cumulus high
as raised elbows in the window
across Railroad Avenue, hair falling
to the floor in Al's barber shop,
qualities scissored away. Sparrows
flutter up from the third rail
like angel voices to inhabit our soft
bodies, 700 Volts.

It was whiteness all around you,
the bandage of your trepanned skull.

I watch a father kissing his infant's sour cheek,
the Egyptian driver of North Star Taxi
blowing steam from coffee, his fogged window
weeping for the blackness of tires
thrown near tracks, his breath like smoke
rising from camps at the Jordanian border.

White the background of numbers
on a telephone dial, the fleece
of eburine clouds, your boyhood
on its back in Astoria Park,
witnessing the sky.

The Korean girl wakens to someone
squawking on the conductor's box:
"You're watching me? Who's watching you?"
her red sports jacket no longer roseate,
white phallus of Parliament Lights
gouging into the dumpster filled with hemlock clippings
and plain dirt,

                    the oxidized steel tower
twisted with ivy like an Ancient
exposing his infant,

cruciform windows in mausoleums,
drained crucifixes, unredness, narrow nothings,
the car seat on the slope, its coils unsprung,
Prestone jugs oozing something green.

The priest's alb as he lifted his arms
to praise the rooms a god saved for our souls,
bony rooms white as teeth.

Buildings boarded up. Burned-out.
A fat man walking fast, pumping his arms
up 125 Street, yesterday's store roof
collapsing onto shoppers below, shattered
glass loud as plunked piano keys,
the flash of water from open hydrants
lost where sound swallows light in the secret life
of tunnels, overhead bulbs, lit arrows,
we're under the city.

White the anger you emitted on your breath,
trapped in snow the blank mystery
of your smile, the clean linen
of your friends that you did not bloody,
all you touched a platinum powder
spilling into rivers, the pallor of
thirty pills you swallowed on 14th Street.

               Underground men
dimly seen on platforms, men in tiny offices
with sooted windows, "Cab→" chalked on a brick
wall, fluorescent strips vivid as nerve
flickering where leaf-rustle of the north-
bound train defies hard girders,
this clinking, this clash, this thrum
of genial darkness
               my arms full of lilies.

EMMA'S LOSS OF HEARING

That small artery to the small bones,
eighty years of blood: tiny hammers
that tap a heard voice, the soughing trees,
an inhabited code you awakened to,
smiling, the pink coverlet drawn to your chin.

    A hiss. An emptiness
like the inside of a fruit: dark,
your husband's mouth opening and closing,

        collapsed flower,
the way stars implode, after momentary redness,
drawn into themselves, your husband's words gone back
down, swallowed.

There, he must have said, "there,"
pointing to his left ear, then at yours,
as if diaphanous demons had flitted across,
their mosquito-songs what you feel entering your blood,
and what taking out, what silence.

Splash of water. Thermostat's "click."
A storm door thumping when you feel the blast
of cold air. Vibrations through your shoes,
a truck going past, the smell of diesel exhaust.

A chickadee's at the feeder,
snatching sunflower seeds;
now he's on the birch branch,
pecking one between his feet.
You can feel him on the back of your hand,

and your husband tapping you,
until you turn, learning the shape of his lips.

"Emma."

ON THE BLACKNESS OF SIDNEY

The first day he came to us, he was outside,
on the ledge, staring through the picture window,
burrs clinging to his haunches, patches of fur missing,
mad with hunger and dermatitis, fugitive from the woods,

accusing us, pressing his soundless cry against glass.
He ran off. Next day, we saw him beneath the blue spruce,
his body absorbed into the darkness of the ground,
eyes like lights risen from a depth. We knelt, and called,

saved him from a diet of crickets, removed swollen ticks,
black blood bursting over thumbnails, spoke to his
survivor's nervousness, arguing a world safe, where love
growls in every tree, mercy squeals, the heart fails.

We saved him again as we returned from the beach,
the smell of sand and sea clinging to towels
and folding chairs. He came limping toward us, wincing
at our touch, panting like an old miner with black lung.

His bladder blocked. Those little stones
accreted from his ashy fears, anger's alkali unfulfilled,
he would soon bloat like a child dying of hunger,
acting out the news of crop failures, helpless,

empathic. The vet removed his penis.
A urethra now wide, to pass the sediments of maleness,
made him no more female than Ethiopian marble
or the altered bulls of Pamplona. That didn't matter.

What astonished was his reaction to the anesthetic:
his balding stomach; a grayish pink showing between
his incipient nipples. It was knowing he wasn't ebony
to his bones. It was the soft feel of his baby skin,

the gradual, darkening fuzz of his body's assumptions,
the way he pulled at his fur, combing it with his teeth,
the tips of white hairs like slivers of moon-fire
flickering in the space between his golden eyes.

A HOUSE

"Where do these children play?" he asks.
"In the halls," a mother tells him.
"Do you get any privacy?"
"Sometimes I sit in the bathroom."
"What do you dream of?"
"I would love a house, a nice house
with chandeliers."

Without the hacking cough of children,
    their inflamed hearing and passive
        silences.

Without 27th Street's
    onion-breathing clerks,
    their raw eyes,

coca leaves dipped in leaded gasoline,
    cigarettes lit in darkness,
    flames eating the broken-spring settee,

without the juice of politicians running down your thighs,
    the white gloss on the edge of photos,
    the gash of light, the convulsion of your body's
        rent,

your name the manufacturer's label on chrome,
your breath the slow asthma of nicotiana,
your bent back an arch of traveled sky,

such crystals would they be, cut tear drops,
    faceted and gleaming,

such nightsticks as branches make, scraping at the window,
    the moon hung from its aluminum post,

your stomach the darkest chamber of the Taj Mahal,
    empty and forbidden.

ON THE EXTRACTION OF EILEEN'S WISDOM TOOTH

What kindness of nature,
  to bury spare parts so deep in bone.
What wear and tear, this biting
  and grinding. Pain in the distal region of speech,
near the jaw's hook, the breaking of four roots
  that snap like popsicle sticks.

                              It was almost
a dream. Sodium pentothal, syringe of Lethe,
  a quick burning in the crook of the elbow,
blue veins bringing back to the heart
  sweet touch, the excruciating twinge of
chocolate.   Taste: an outward-bulging heat, a nerve
  threaded to a corner of the eye, as if winking
made one salivate, and time looped back upon us,
changing scenes. I'm the man in white jacket, holding
                                    x-rays
against the kitchen light, tsk-tsking, smacking my lips
  with disappointment.   Hugeness you feel near your left
cheek: a fact you can't swallow. Pain's second heart
  your throbbing mandible, a hush working toward the ear.
Dry lips. Damp forehead. White pill. The afternoon
  exposed to the bone. I think only of pink veal.
      A small, bloody fist closing.

THE EXPULSION

We look over our shoulders,
arms lifted as if dropping
a great burden, bellies rounded
from the garden's bounty, lean,
pale, beautiful as the angel
driving us away.
                The puzzle is not
our lack of aureole—his flat
golden halo identical to God's,
seen as we face Him
approaching from an irritated
distance—but why we're not alarmed
at going or staying, speechless in birdsong
air, placid as angels are meant to be.

God is moving toward us,
rolling the wheel of Creation
like a plate of concentric and varying
blues, upheld by seven winged heads
that must be angels lacking bodies,
my hand pointing at the verge
that is East, obscuring your
breast, the angel pushing
us past seven narrow trees
twining upward like ironwood,
the entrance to your womb a folded shadow.

His leg's bent at the knee,
sprinter's calf curved
as the apples in spiked
leaves above our heads,
decoratively glowing,
puckered around their stems

like hindquarters of sleeping
animals in configurations of gray
resolved into salamanders.
We are looking into his sibling eyes,
we are caught among flowers,
stepping on five-hundred-year-old
scarlet vegetation, four serpents
streaming, a *trompe l'oeil*
oozing toward hillock or pit,
three strides jeopardized
by God's wheel bearing down upon us.

We've misjudged the angel.
He wants us to stay,
thin hand on my shoulder
twisting me toward the edge
of his halo, an encroaching
dark circumference.
Your face becomes furrowed,
your hand bends upward,
warding off a blow at the border,
though you, too, turn
toward his loneliness.
Any minute there might never be
the small scar above your lip,
my mole removed with electric
needle, sadness on Davidson Avenue,
sparrows plucking bread from fire
escapes, your letters from Indiana.

We shall never button our daughter's coat,
climbing the snowy hills of Syracuse.

REFIGURATIONS

*(after an exhibit of recent painting
from Germany)*

Shades of sun daubed like make-up
beneath the eyes. A sameness.
Baselitz's women hanging upside-down,
almost always blonde, the skeletal church
each side of them what's left
of a grasp flensed to the bone,
and upstairs, the lemon-colored land
too far from sea, too grainy
between the burned-out Panzer tanks.
Though the serpent curling toward
sleeping *Paganini* is golden,
the swastikas floating from the musician's nose
are not. Musical notes like little
death's-heads.
                     One goes to whiteness.
And black. Greta Garbo facing
Erich von Stroheim, madonna and magus;
charcoal-limned Warhol and Mussolini
cartoon-serious, flat wings of a triptych,
as we fracture and reassemble
around something American,
something red,
something splayed like the painter
   dead in a phone booth:

the moon hanging its canary lozenge
over a scarlet city,
    pelicans with green wings thrashing the air,
    partly air-borne, their bodies dripping from the dark
river,

      flames leaping from the wire
      trash basket in Tompkins Square Park

(on the way home, reading Rilke's
"*Kindheit*," mother's fingers
sliding across the piano's white keys,

      Harlem skidding past,
      the train rushing north).

Consonants in titles
escape translation
where g's go mad with diaspora
and loneliness
and violence   homage
      to van Gogh at the wall,
      to greenness at the Bahnhof,
      to the gagging reflex in
      Café Deutschland IV,
          barbed wire, stone, tape recorders,
          binoculars, mushroom-shaped lamps,
          long coats, *die Polizei*,

flickering ruby glow of an auto burning.

THINKING OF GUSTAV KLIMT,
WITH MOLLY ON MY LAP

It is her favored cat's position: kneading me
with her clawless pads, purring, her green
reptilian eyes studying white words on the PC screen,
waiting for her name to appear. Her pupils dilate.
Rain lashes against the window.
                               A whir of gold
in my mind; a woman emerging, as from a gold-leaf
quilt, extruded, bare-breasted, a metallic tapestry
what the world becomes behind her, the bursting of
body cells into their elements: auric arrangements
of eyes, silvery traces of an artisan's fingers,
Molly pushing paws into my velour shirt, imprinting it,
licking the white border of her natural white ruff,
now crossing her white paws, suddenly quiescent,

            and Klimt's *The Kiss* begins
to glow in a crowded room, where men and women
jostle politely, perfume mingled with nicotine,
eyes flashing,
            where man and woman fuse into a column
of weightless colors, the woman's uplifted face leaning
into her left shoulder, his hands stroking her cheek,
her temple; tendrils coiled around her ankles, for she
is on her knees, where he is simply phallic, emerging
from a ground of broken glass,
                         and Molly begins
kneading again, the rain at forty-five degrees
against the window, kitchen vent clanking in the wind,

            and it's Klimt's *Salome* holding
John the Baptist's head, her fingers supple as young bone,
his closed eyes like a man's grown tired of reading,
no blood here, no redness, just her brownish nipples,
broken spirals, caught currents of air, her profile
ecstatic,

        and Molly getting bored, looking at these words,
my hands clicking the space bar at the keyboard,
Molly turning in my lap, her paws on my chest, moving
rhythmically toward my throat, while she pushes into velour,
into the dry silence of a darkening room.

FIVE CATS AND A DISCUSSION OF THE SOUL, AFTER A TRIP TO SOUTH CAROLINA

Gradations of light.
Shadows moving across a Lenox vase.
Something stationary in white tufts
of pampas grass, sea oats,
the rasping edge of palmettos:
                              the soul is
like a porous crustacean
that moves from body to body,
though it escapes
the outline of its temporary housing
like the water snake
slithering out of its skin,
the crackling envelope draped over a rock,
eye-holes a clarity
in diaphanous cessation.

It was safe to grow abstract
where one could count
the joggers slapping along wet sand,
the corn cobs spilling from trash bags,
the number of streams that drain tobacco fields,

to dream of living
in rented cottages that leaned back
from sea-walls, with names like *Wild West, Ampersand, Typhoon,*

while our much-traveled cats
occupied damp couches, sprawled on a sandy rug
in their various postures,
licking and smoothing out a ruffled haunch,
gagging up a hairball,
                      dozing with paws folded like hands,

lips twitching,
                united to their natures
as easily as the tropisms of the sunflower
lift a yellow-hived face to the light.

Surely, we can be home now, where snow
drifts over the porch steps,
the town plow rumbles in the darkness.

   We still hear the traffic of US 17:
                feel a motion in the blood
crossing the Pee Dee and Santee Rivers,
gathering momentum in sleep,
                          eager
for the approaching curve
of the sea, the school of porpoises, the black
humps revolving out of salt, wheeling back in.

READING THE *TIMES* IN THE CAR WASH

It's like entering the belly of an apocalyptic
beast, while it sleeps,
limp brushes hanging down, undigested
forms of sea life,
                the boy, its prisoner,
taking coins, scrubbing road salt from rear
lenses, stabbing at our hubcaps.

We read of teetering stocks,
the Middle East. I look at bodies of gassed
Kurds, I count pictures of the homeless,
bull's-eye upright bears in a shooting gallery,
bing, bing, I can hear the crack of .22's,
casings hit the floor.   And the brushes come alive,
the yellow ones on each side,
buffing our doors, folding back the sideview mirrors,
catching the rear wiper arm that sticks out
like a compound fracture,
                        the muddy ooze
washing down the windshield,
all this hissing, flashing of lights
telling when wax spurts all over us
like sperm, premature,
the beast coming into itself,
as we proceed,

    fingers darkened with politicians
pounding the podium, soldiers
beating a boy, burnoosed men
throwing missiles,
                  the fine spray
fanning along the car,
dancing strips of chamois
dragging overhead,

      here's ul-Haq blown to bits,
      Bangladesh 3/4th's flooded
where every minute's lost
to the Ganges, Jamuna, and Meghna
Rivers,

the centrifugal-stiff
fibers of the wheeling brush
drooping behind us like post-hurricane
trees on the Cayman Islands,
as we emerge with chrome into sunlight,
dropping quarters into the damp boy's cup,
speeding down Route 52 without a care in the world.

LES AMOUREUX EN VERT

I am resting my head on your clavicle;
the white ruff at your shoulder must be
   a small kitchen valence.

     You are stiff as a board,
hair dyed black, your eye like coal,
my lips faintly purple from lack of air.
We have stopped breathing for ourselves,

the numbness of your profile like a wife's
   at the pyre before sati,

     your lips parted,
my closed crescent eyelid and ashen face
suited to sleep somewhere below Bucharest,
bitter cold, my hat blown away at the train station
   where I leave for the Black Sea.

Behind us, this ink-stained baize,
folded felt one smooths out before cutting
an exact circle to fit the base of a fluted
brass lamp:

   a crumpled field to be snapped taut,
pasted level to accommodate billiards and
     cigars smoldering on mahogany ledges.

     Take this
blotchy darkness that occupies the unseen
portion of our profiles, where vinyl
extension cords fray in third-floor rooms
in Brooklyn, and heaters explode,

         and time
exposes the flat side of our heads

the way a young lieutenant opens
the lid of an aunt's ebony box:

   take this roundness
of your breast, my completely missing torso,

everything Western and white, Islamic,
Judaic, everything powdered like ancient
mortar at a wailing wall that has sifted
into pigments and roughened our lying down.

WAVING TO MR. ROMNEY

Seasonal dice flung once more:
on line in 7–11, defying
February, packing 16 oz. coffee,
buttered roll; the frozen lot outside
nothing but a mind's rippled gray
that will not thaw with words,
Chinook jargon, *skookum*, faint
resemblances to skua, winged predators
of ice, or jaegers, whatever one calls
heartland and power. Traffic backs up.
An engine squeak-squeaks, standing still.

Who wouldn't be somewhere else,
waving from a ferry in the BVI,
rocking toward Tortola, greeted
by you, Clinton Romney, father of
five? Your taxi a flatbed truck
with candy-striped canopy. Eyes
trained to distance. Daughters gone
to St. Thomas, New York, college
degrees. They are borrowings of anthurium,
bougainvillea, this hospital
and prison, Road Town's cousins
to sooty stone and brick
that children see for themselves:
clinging to straps in subways,
measuring the harbor's curve
by whiteness of ads,
a blank sea without tide, a job.

I'm backing out, these gaps
in ice like the missing molars
of your smile. I'm pulling north
with coffee and the *Times*,

the front-page sadness of your face,
your paunchy gestures,
your hand that lingers in the air
and turns palm up,
>   what-can-one-do-
>   the-life-here-
>   they-do-not-want,
>   my children.

I'm plunging down 100,
sputtering past
Primrose Elementary School.
No pigtails or yellow
uniforms. No stony-faced
domestics in white
back from Charlotte Amalie,
sons like foam, caught between
Beef Island and northern
shale. A gentle person serves
tea. Here's Guana Island,
Scrub, Great Camanoe,
miles of blue air, Puerto Rico,
the great blue-green
water, your turquoise depth
bewildered by its
clarity.

from *Curve Away from Stillness* (1989)

CHEMISTRY

      1

Shifting:
          his driveway
          rutted with ice
  the double
     Norway spruce
    leaning
   split trunks in the wind:
     water
          like the season
sufficient
    and
divided   hardening
   into elements where green
          combines
        a salt
        with the coldness in his
     voice   as if the brick house
    the red
  and regular crystal
        of
          an opposing
            solid
              burned
        off
like a vapor
        damp wood
        hissing
     in the airtight stove
while he watered the almost dry
       draecena
        his mood
     altering

without warning
without a knowledgeable drift
                    as though he were a blind skier being
lifted
    swaying on a hook

                        told of the slope's
condition   imagining the shock to his ankles
                    when he landed

            the shuddering sightless
        downhill run   surface and temperature
                not of the room he was
        in   then suddenly
                returned to
                                this trembling in his legs
though he stood still   though he stared at the light
            breaking through gray webbing of the birch tree
    visibly
at least
himself   in this time   the place of his
                    choosing   habiliment in white
            winter's habitual breathless
                        hibernation the illusion
                                            of stasis

and
    upstairs
                        in the red-
            carpeted study
                between shelves
                of Renaissance
                books

            redness in the walls
            as in tapestries
            and doublets of princes

                        his wife worked on her novel
    her typewriter

    rearranged the evening
          into summer   when a
                                              glass
                          of water
                  sweating
            between his hands
                    was a solute
                warmer
        than darkness
         drawn from wells

when the vertical
blinds of his living room
were not
  the companionable
shadows of stripped
           trees
                       a broken lattice of crystals

                        though
                        the overhead island
                        of sky
      the sunset
                  were now the separable
                  admonitions
                     of an early
                  moon

and the road
worn through its yellow
lines
brought a blackness
            he could explain
                  as the imprint
                  of an evening
                  without backyard
                lights   without the acrid
                air of chimneys

                     without a center he exchanged
                              heat
                                 from
       his wife's sentences
         the work
            added to a system
                                                to their marital
                                   grid

                              as if separation
                                 elongated
   the orbit of their
   shared
   life   and something
                        sharp
            assailed
         the outermost
   swing
            of his senses
                                          (a boy's cry
         where ammonia splashed on the bathroom wall
         breath seared to the base of his lungs' capacity)

               could he be that young
      again   could he
           inhale the same mixture
                                          of old porcelain
   and damp towels   could he inhibit an
                                       insidious heat
                  loss   listening to the sibilance
                           of waxed skis

         was he going at such a rate
                     down   or towards
   whatever loosened into
                     time   a
                              never completed
                        reaction

   so that
   he could
       imagine harmonies
                  of an old
                           Philco
               where steam knocked
          in silver
       radiators
        and he remembered
     his mother crooning   a noise in his sleep
                                in the walls
              like the mourning of doves

              2

     But there could be just so much
              heat   if he were himself
                   a
        system
                 just so much loss of
     heat   a certain maximum
        death   as if his entropic increase
   were the fictive need of a fictive past
imagined
           movement in his standing
still
                something
            affixing itself
   in precise measure
to the available niche
     of a quantized
orbit   as if a man weeping
      could not
  hear
  himself
    above the howl of wind   the rattling
                   window pane
   but knew the sound

                    was there
                                        a steady static
                              posited
                    (as just now his wife's
               characters
     gathered in a parking lot
          sizing each other up

                         he warned himself
                    not to get out of the car
                         he had so
          furtively
               backed into the darkness beneath
                                             a tree   trying
          to emerge
like a subsidiary
walk-on   knowing surely something of himself
               must be there
     their life rushing into each
small silence
                    while she progressed
through the conflicts
          of her people   the rising inflection
                    of the woman's voice as she turned
          to her male companion
                    in her old
               Mercedes   the steering just a little
     loose   the man's response sufficiently
          subliminal   so that the plot might
                                        be advanced
when they climbed the rocks above her grandfather's
                                        mansion)

and here he was turning
inward   his wife's keys
               clacking like an instrument
counting
isotopes in the medium of his advance

        or backward
   progress   his thoughts colorless and rare

  (the woman pointing to her
                     Mercedes
which was after all   as she explained
       battered
                 saying to the man
   atop an igneous crest   the mansion small
                          so far below
or was it gneiss
or schist   that he mistook her for someone of his
                              own
invention)

    something as astonishing
  as the
  intake
of the lungfish's
        innovative
      breath

   as if the boy
       he once was
            had exhaled
               doubt from his
hearing   as if he now slipped
          from his dreams
             like a newly gilled
        mammal
down the muddy
bank
           and could measure
                 the moral
           volume of
  an
    emptiness
of heart
so easily

occupied   it seemed
wrong
          he should be
happy
               remembering that job   the white
                                    uniform
          the plant behind smokestacks on the shore of a
                                              river
                               where vats swirled and he
                         added
               caffeine and caramel
               color
     to darken an invert
sugar   clouding a shifting
clear column
               the way his mind
          swirled
          now   (what
                               might the man
               be saying as the woman tossed
                    her hair back with defiant
               eroticism   the air soft
  in a contrary
          landscape of ironwood
                    and shagbark hickory

          what if he himself went upstairs
with tea   the offer of a light
               winsome
                    snack
               introducing an unknown
     free
     energy to a system she was trying to close
               without him)

                         but if her
language
                    dictated

                        the exact
                    temperature
                at which reactants
gave up their
natures   then his inward
                        song
was the hum
drawn up
through a chemist's
hood   issuing
                    into the air
                as toxic
                    excess
                where he wanted facts to be like lock
                                    and key
where he peered through
    prisms   an intruder
            into his own
future   as if instruments
        straightened his lines
    of intent   as if his soul
were the floating
                disk
            of orange
            light
                that would not
                    coincide
                with a paler
                trembling twin

3

Tonight he would be
        glass
            he would flow
        imperceptibly
                he would be so clear
                    the soft crystals of

                              self
                  would unlatch
                their closed
   facets   would release the infinitesimal
                  voltages
             that bound voice to
                     an actual
                     throat
             as he stepped through the back door
                              the porch light
                     circumscribing
 where he stood   not where
                he might walk
not where he might
be within
her hearing
             not to alter the appearance
                of mansions
    the arrival of
             geese

(not to think
    it was right they should talk of families
             with her girlhood home
 in sight   the plot eddying
    that carried them
                away
    the woman tying up her hair
        while that man broke off a branch of the wing tree
      confessing
    there was something in nature he could not
trust
                as if   she said   you had a
choice)

not where the edge existed
    between freezing and burning   table salt
                              ticking

                      on the icy stairs
like the sound of sand
blowing onto a windshield

                      the sound of desert wind
            when
      he had driven so far
     west   in that time
        before they met

   (it would seem
 sophistical
              if I said I choose
     to be here   with you

he kicked loose a tussock
of grass
                 and she blushed
he thought
        ever so faintly)

if there could have been
such a time

       the job
that had almost burned the hands off
an ignorant worker   *naphtha and fire*
            what could a man believe
      about water and air   *yes*
he knew chemicals   *and they paid him*
    a short bus ride
      an absurd loneliness
  in
  the rubber mask
that protected his eyes
    his breath filtered by the cannister
strapped to his chest
  that allowed him
to function while others emerged

  coughing
        air force jets
booming through the sound
barrier
     (everything in nature
is ours   she said it
with such conviction
   he laughed)

What
even now
 would
 cool his
  gloved
  hands
so
quickly
as the bath of anhydrous
    ammonia what would
        slide
  so easily as water
 from teflon
   explode
like bars of sodium
 in the sea *what would*
   survive
solitude
where a train
 whistle
pierced long
 evenings
in Culver City
his boyish letters home
 constructed
wishfully
as a telluric
 helix
    elements

*arranged
in the wistful
success
of cylinders   their curves
and extensions
his love of separations
like discredited
numbers
erased from a chart

periodic
as friendships

as the appearance of palm trees

the gleam
of sunlight
on the black hood
of an old
Dodge with
stiff steering

his progress down
Sepulveda
Blvd   himself ridiculing
the time devoted to
Werther's sorrows
an Indonesian worker
showing him
scars from a Japanese
bayonet   all these semi-
colloids
of his
perception   semen of unknown
and un-
founded
attractions   as if love
could be learned*

        from
    the kindness
in a
     voice   *from the landlord's*
                        wife
            who visited his green
            cottage

                        4

And now
the floodlight
like an alien
          sun   so far
                  from that time
  it seemed not to reveal huge fir trees
each side of the driveway
                        a star
        of the smallest magnitude
     combusting
his past   his shadow
        thrown on gravel frozen
into ruts   where he turned
           to confront
                a coldness
           in himself   as if long
chains of carbon
  an endless series of hydrogen
     bonds   culminated
       in the low temperatures at which the self
became a superfluid
           oozing through microscopic
flaws
        his reasons
     for apartness
      a slow
unlikely burning

      without heat   as if he could ignite like water
                  in fluorine gas
like asbestos
like glass   a skin dissolving
from which he stepped
                                    out
          of himself
entirely   her typing
  the most natural
        sound
            in the lit stillness

(the man and woman returned
        months later to the same
hill   his hangdog look
evidence of what he had argued so vehemently
against in her
      though he refused to call it
conscience   what then
            what then
she demanded   his loyalty
                  decidedly not
          the issue
though a war was on   though a priceless tapestry
    had disappeared   and she
stopped short of embracing him
    because   )

these variables
then
  would always
matter: where he was
     and with what need
    his mind
  traveled
      to what other place
        what fever brought new
conductivity to his
blood

What metalloid
  barely re-
   active
        harmonies
   filled the slanted
            space
       between
  the noise of the woman next door
  and news of illness
three thousand
miles away   three lifetimes
removed along the equator that was
    like a thin strand
of uncoiled
   genetic
material   a dark sliver or shadow
between hemispheres   as if voice could be ductile
and reflective
      could dissolve
in the Mississippi
or Colorado
      Rivers
to arrive
basic
     as floating
   oxides   the text
of his mother's
       letter
    like a newspaper
held over
flame   beginning to brown
           in his
         thoughts   an application
of heat he had harbored
         like style
heaviness
          impediment
   in the construction

of foreign
   syllables   *as in humid evenings*
                  as in the call
of flamboyant
   screeching birds

              (because even in his response
there would be implicit
   rejection   and she feared
        something ulterior with so much
                money involved
     or was it power
  he sought   his attitude as he lay back
               on withered grass
   suggesting neither lassitude
nor cunning   she almost
            relented)

What his mother described
   in her graceful script
  not reversible
          nor could there be less
passion for disorder
even in someone as controlled
as he   *his life a sudden phosphorous*
          flaring
    alchemical   *as if from dried*
       urine and sand
   a simple heat
could produce light   *a version*
        of integrity

           (the typing ceased
  her shadow
  moving
across the drawn shade   her voice
calling down   so that he
   heard her just as he was

         entering the cellar
                              and shouted where he
was)

He
had been able to reconstruct
the scene from her
sentences
                                       the indoor
                    lighting and
                                  discoloration
                    of his father's
                                  embalmed
hand   that spot
                         showing through cosmetic
                    clay   the deep oxidation
of chemical
hunger   the sunken tissue
                                around the closed
         eyes   the hair arranged
                                       to conceal
                         sutures and re-
                                  arrangements
                         the fracture
                    of organs
         death
neatly laid out
in ruffles   the polished handles
                    from which a grasp would slide
              back toward daylight
the dull
      progress
   that would continue
in the ground   where the body yields
              its metals
   where the movement down
                    toward increased
                              malleability

                                in
                                    an
                            undiscovered
                                        copper
                                is the slow
        accretion
                of freed elements
                                at decay's
                electrode   as if a son's
                                        reduction
                        and crumbling
                            anger
        his refusal to appear at a nonevent
                        were not loss
                            but the gain of new
                negatives   the undoing
                                of habitual
                        affirmations   where motion
                                is the random song
                        of ions   his blood
                                        a solvent
                                        for
                                    compounds
                                        of
                            language
                                        the long night
                                        a potential
            disharmony   a loosening darkness

                            dawn
        a storm of particles   brightening the surface
                                        of ordinary
                                        chromes
                            in toasters
    the legs of formica tables
                                decorative strips on the doors of old
                                                Buicks
                    rings of looseleaf binders

                    a nimbus
    seen around
                            cups
            and the small
            heads
                        of
            chickadees
                                    so that he could have been going
                                                                    blind
                                            he could have
                                    summed
    himself
                            into the
                                    space
                            between
                                    protons and
                                            neutrons   perfectly
                                                        miming
                                    the nothing
                                            that is
                                    matter

                                    5

"What are you doing?"
                                    the kitchen
so bright he put his hands to his
eyes   she hugged
him   "Your ears are so
        cold!"
    He grinned
                    he kept grinning
and
she yelped
when he rubbed his chin's
            stubbly chill
        into her neck
and he apologized and made

```
            tea
                              they
                         talked
         her last
    chapter would be         perhaps
                                              a
                            marriage
    of some kind
                         did he like that
    conclusion?
                         he wanted to explain
                     himself
         as a habit
            of surface
                                 liable
    to evaporation
                         how the pressure of light
                            her mere
                         walking
    toward the door
                        was
                            an affair
                    of motion in the cosm
    mirroring
                         a joy
                            new
    conversions of loss
                    the union
                         of her
              art with
              his random
    edges
         where solids would
                  flow     where the transformation
                       of never empty
                       or shapeless
                            space
```

                              would be the working
                of a mouth
                                    his fingertips
                      scarred from acids
                      leaving crisscrossed
                            whorls
                         in contact
                            with
                      her smooth arm

did he like that idea?
                                    Oh
                  she was so
total   he said
and they talked
            while the plum
brandy
     slurred its way
home   while she
       grew sleepy

                his emergence
            from the kitchen
              after
            she went
upstairs to bed   saying
            don't be long

                      the impossible release of mass
                                  and energy
                                  from a closed
                                  system
                  the triggering
                        enzymes of his sight
                              nothing
                              to why he turned
                                        his head
                                    upward to the
                        stars arranged like clarities

                        like isolate
                qualities
of cold and attraction

                        why
                                on the downward slope
                                        of Dogwood Lane
                as he walked between the plowed ridges
                                of the road
                the southern
                        border of his
                   land
                he knew the rhythmic
                                gravity
                of her
breathing
                                of her fluttering eyelids
                of her sleep-
                        worn syllables
                shaping his name
                                                miraculously

BIOLOGY

                              1
                    There is only this
     steel bridge rusted out

         fishermen's
         flat-bottomed
         boats upended
         on a muddy slope   swans congregating
                                    on Muscoot reservoir
              the western hill
                   you call your mountain

              this overcast
                   day's
              blank
     Pepsico
         building
              squaring off a rounded
                   shoreline   stone and glass
                        supplanting
                   trees
                   stripped of bark by white-tail
              deer   there is only
                        our blood
              converging   our mixed
                   inheritance of dirt from Irish
     farms
     the fields of Krk   eons of insensate
                                              stone
                        angular unconformities
                                         of Being
                   imitating granite and
                        basalt   heaved
                   into a dream of
                             Adriatic air

we are
here   we are here
in the smallest fold
          of unborn
               leaves

               turning off the road
                    behind our house
watching a haggard hawk
                    swoop to her
                    survival

a wound occurring
among pines
          in there the small
     scream   the sudden
                    death

                    the cud
               of a violent cosmos
                    spewed into the eventual
                         coolness of a peony's
                    interior
                         the scarlet peony here
                         simply to be here
                              again   as the yellow
                                   finch is here
                         on our wide-mesh fence
                         that protects New Guinea impatiens
                    from the dog   the finch
                              here above the hidden
                                   blackness of the cat
                                   in the cool hostas
               the finch singing
where I dig up plantain
          from the driveway
                         where sparrows scour
     the naked stone

                    for seed   dandelions rooted between
                                            broken cinder blocks
                                                and brick   the beige
                                    spider suddenly the exact color
                                            we have painted
                                                    our garage
                the finch and his
                mate   flying the curve of a sine wave
                            up
                    into the storm-broken
                        branch of a maple   into
                                                                opportunity
                                        above the cat
                                        and spider

                                        2

        Opposite Daufuskie Island
                                            Calibogue
                                            Sound yields
                            to the open sea
                                                exhausted
                where we harvest
                        a low tide's
                            display
                                            the sea cucumber opening
                                                her tentacles
                                                    in the plastic cup we fill
                                                with water
                            sister to the hydra
                                    listen
                        listen   we might
                                        amble in the twilight
                                    on jointed legs
        our skeletons external   turning knee-deep
                                            in the shallows of the sand bar
                                    we might radiate a more exact

64

··········symmetry··extrude a pharynx
··in the long wash of sunset

··our tanned
··faces uplifted
··to receive the shadows
··of pelicans

the bony parts
and the soft parts········in the green capacity
································of sea lettuce··········making
··selves from
··light and the salty
··secretions of coral
····················and the bequeathed movement of the first
································alga into a puddle
································that dried into land
··where we might have been
································blue-green
································or brown or red

········plants
········hungry for the touch
························of beetle legs
························on trigger hairs
········snapping shut spiny lobes
········while we slowly digest
························death and grow
························alert to the purposes
························of hardness············the long projection of
··the horseshoe crab's
··spine
··············like a weapon
····································a deadly dart

····that we see it
····dig
····into the
····sand to
····upright itself

··its carapace later

                                        a thin
                                 crackling papyrus
                                  in the dog's jaws

what would we do clinging and sedentary in a moist habitat
what would we think facing each other across minute distances
like the barely distinguishable parts of moss or the chipped
pine cone that has come to rest beneath pink and yellow zinnias

what amphibian lurch of the backbone takes us into the compost
where the tortoise lays her eggs and the small cadavers of
toads have been flung by the mower's blades what would we assert as
ours as desire is ours as the distinct cavity of the mouth is ours

                              3

                       We have come
to this
particular
    strip
       of Sea Pines Plantation   not to forget the twin
                                         bridges into Charleston
                                         and the fright of traveling
                                         thin steel over so much
                                             harbor

                                      not to forget the ladies
                                          weaving sweet
                                            grass into baskets
                                           among cut flowers
                                      in front of a circular
                                             church
not to be able to say
a Gullah sentence and
know nothing of black women
who live by the quick twinings of their fingers
         who walk on sand
   between washed-up

    reeds and razor-sharp
      burrs   carrying life
        on the surface of pain

                        not to believe the blind
                        life of plants
                        could be
                        unthinkingly
                  ours

*   not to be*
*   automatic*
*   as filter-feeding*
*   mosquito larvae*
* beating a current*
*   into their*
*   gullets*

*   the earthworm*
*   grinding particles*
in its gizzard
*   not to know*
*   the backward-curved teeth of the snake*
holding down what is already a bulge in the body
*   though everywhere*
*   a need to take*
within
*   to have out-there*
*   become*
*   where will begins*
*   as the hunger of oxygen*
*   entering blood   whispering*
*   through the spiracles*
*   of grasshoppers*
*   into the stomata of shade-loving*
* trees*
*   the action of any orifice*
*   a sentience   a decision*
*   selection a kind of*

pleasure
in momentum

                        the way we drove
                          to Bogue Island
                          and watched the lightning's
                            jagged plunge
                            sever the sky
                          to make our flooded
                          route rich in ozone
felt it entering
        our pores
    when we parked at Starvin' Marvin's
                letting the sky carry its load
                of darkness south from Hatteras
        as if there had to be just so much
        of it out there in the distance
        to shade the cornfields
to move us closer
to each other   to balance
                    light and salt
                    in the clear lymph
                    that flows
              between the heart's
            pulse and the first
entry of something
into a wound   that was the sky
                     itself
          that was the white-capped water of Atlantic
          Beach
and the next day's clear weather
through Emerald Isle   the gouged woods
                          where condominiums
                     proliferated
                            like organisms

and we talked of sulfur dioxide
used to kill the wild yeasts

                that spoil wine   we sang our road
                                                                songs
                        spilled the last coffee
                                from a broken thermos
                felt the air
    moving against us
                        twisting through the vents
                                sliding along the outer
                                        surface of our
                                                human
                        volume

                                        4

                Home
    here it is
    home   tiered slope of orange cosmos and white phlox
    again   again
            the swollen pods of sweet
                        william   long-necked
                                succulents   low-lying
                                        blue
                        ageratum along the slate-walk

                                nothing
    nothing
    calls in dialect
    so truly
    as the wood thrush
                marking his particular
                        tree
                    his thin border
                    like our
    Dogwood Lane between
    a neighbor revving
    his open-throated
    Trans-Am and me
    hurtling on the tractor

    downhill behind the peach trees
        all this roaring
each side of a street   all this singing
          from the mulberry tree struggling up
        between Douglas firs

      all this counterpoint
of bird and bird
          magnolia and mimosa
        the separate tangles
          of caged harmonies   of blown
blossoms and just emerging puffs
of scarlet   up there in the mimosa something like
sea anemones   the hummingbird darting across her
        habitat
    into the dilated dusk
      of our eyes

where the Japanese beetles fall into a plastic bag
duped by synthetic mating scent   by the pheromone
        that brings them
      copulating in the peach-colored roses
        where I pluck them in pairs
          crack them between thumb
            and forefinger
        in this August
      afternoon
    when I would seek the ants that
      stroke aphids
        to milk for their
           honeydew

I would see the round dance
  and the waggle dance
      of bees   I would tell you
            just how distant
        our food is from the hive
          how many meters

             my instinct travels
                  to attract
                     your
                    touch
             where you tie up
                 wandering
        morning-
glory's
           mauve trumpets

from *Scenarios for a Mixed Landscape* (1986)

LEGEND OF THE MINIATURE ROSE

    Frost sometimes fails
where talus accumulates its angle of debris
    degrees at a time, the year's steep
hypotenuse between mountain and plain. It was here
    that Colonel Roulet, far from the village,
found the flower no larger than his infant daughter's
    soul. Its thorns hardly a prickle,
he dropped to his knees, cradled it, blew on the frail
    ember of its mouth. At this height,

beyond shadows of creaking wheels and the heavy breath
    of oxen, so close to the tarn,
and cirque and cup of glacial retreat, the clutched hand
    turns upward, light slides down the slope
like lateral moraine. But he gathered those roots
    to his heart, under layered clothing,
close to his damp heat, where the nipple hardens in
    sudden draughts, and hair curls gray;
he imagined a window box in sunlight, his daughter's

    first words, the steam of soups,
loam crumbling in the darkness, swollen nodules like pink
    knuckles of a tiny grasp. Thus, he descended,
the wind slashing him beyond the sheltering rock, above
    the freeze-line, as he thought he heard
the clatter of chamois and mouflon, and stumbled, and gripped
    the sharp stones. He felt that moist breath
under his shirt, the root-pulse, the head drooping that he
    and his children would water for a hundred years.

BUYING A GIFT FOR LIESL IN BLOOMINGDALE'S

You have a baby brother on the way,
the land swelling where you live in the south
of France, a third language to count the years
before you're five. This spring, the sky here will
not peel back its gray husk, I cannot hear
the mistral rushing through the Rhone valley,
mulched soil beginning to breathe its life so
late I've come to Bloomingdale's to purchase
color for you, godchild, bloom of the sea.

It's no matter which way the missiles point,
not today, among the blue Kashan rugs,
sisals from India, the sun glinting
outside on the bumper of a Rolls Royce,
while young women stop at the cosmetics
counter, arrange the latest angles of
shadow across the eyes, and later sit
on silk modulars, lit by Imari
lamps, catching the light on their polished nails.

One can visit these glass shelves, the pale greens
of porcelain country scenes, the glazed hogs
that do not make a sound like the goat you're
chasing along the stone wall your father
has just repaired. You're letting mother rest,
brother kicking, while the hum of the land
is silent here among the immobile
microwave plastic ware, and I reach toward
ceramic onions, far from Avignon.

FLOWER

Wet morning: the pink verbena is home
from oblivion, its white center wide
as an eye staring at the sea, its own
glitter fallen on the deep, while its stem
stiffens to the root pulled loose from darkness.
I lift my face abruptly to the sun.
At my feet, lobelia, blue as fleawort
and cornflowers, clusters of that color
springing free into the empyrean,
inside this space where thought turns like the wind,
blind as gods chained in caves, sudden in song.

Let men open hands to lift a fragrance
like thin sheets of mist, building cold, clear rooms
we yawn in, rubbing eyes, trenching valleys
in the sun. Dark ribs surround that fire.
Gases flare distant roses, corollas
in telescopes, wherever the clouds race
toward night. I tend my *cardenalis* here
thin as a strip of blood, upright as stone,
and zinnia, balsam, vexed petals, their
trembling horizontals, the drying green
of leaves like lids only the dead see through.

SOUTHERN EXPOSURE

Drought. Everything driving deeper,
        higher. Borers
nipping the crown of new growth
        on the white pine.
Light snapping behind the eyes like
        dry fingers. All
that's left of the rabbit is
        hindquarters,
abandoned by the cat: the rabbit,
        hurtling headlong
out of time, almost making it.

In the palm of my hand, the shallow
        rivulet that divides
my grasp is branching into the air
        around me: blood
echoing a phantom pulse somewhere
        in the moon,
tree toads singing, sudden trill
        of the mockingbird.
A bad smell from the woods. I'm not
        reaching in, where it was
whatever it was, curled up, shredded to the bone.

Painting the siding this high up, I've tied
        the rope to the chimney,
knotted it to my waist, while sun
        blinds me on white
surfaces. I probe into scaled
        gray corners, where
wasps emerge, sticky and writhing
        in wet latex. I don't
look down. They struggle up the slope.
        Fresh ones arrive, circle
my head, their legs dangling, as if to grip my hair.

VARIATION ON HEAT AND SILENCE

Hornets overhead, in a canopy of catalpa bloom,
humming a bass to high notes in the tatter
of my damaged hearing, the hemlock newly sunk
with its balled roots in front of the picture window,

shaped like a Scotch pine, a Christmas tree without ornament;
my back stiff, loose dirt filling my gloves with grit,
the mockingbird swaying on the tip of blue spruce
coaxing me with his bogus cardinal's call into idleness:

on such a day, in the midst of huge labors, the dinosaurs
busy in the far swamps, insects unflexing their wiry legs,
their multi-eyed cubist heads tilted toward interstices of air,
perhaps it was then the sun's sister entered the Oort cloud,

her small red nimbus like the mist a god's messenger arrives in,
and she wooed stray comets out of their fitful orbits,
gave them a new direction, a new union-to-be in the random
curvatures of her dance, and they penetrated the webs

of Jupiter and Saturn, broke through the secondary light of moons
that make their own tides in the ocean-free unending darkness,
and they came in a shower of dust, a great buzzing,
their vivid tails slapping mountains, bending back the trees,

a gray whirlwind melting through clouds of ash, land everywhere
the clay-absorbing hunger, the sludge and bones of reptiles without
    name.

THE BIRTH OF TIME

It must have crystallized in a spiral galaxy
like the darkly glittering neutrons of a twinless
star, skimming along the curve of everything
expanding like lungs, before breath could be,

before the cooled and irregular fistlike chunk of sun
became the ridges of Himalaya, before gases
choked themselves free of oceans. It visited this place
like a comet, the long tail its accumulated force,

where nothing could be amazed, nothing tremble
or shrink with pain. It arrived transparent as bird calls,
hot as fever, pointed to penetrate membranes
and the pulsing wings of dragonflies. It was here,

crowding molecules, linking the twisted chains
of such small secretions it seemed random and trivial,
while sun-flares cauterized the earth's crust,
the land heaved its bowels into the boiling seas.

It grew hungry and afraid, without enemies, without needs,
without a diaphanous sheath, without the filling
of a single vacuole, or something fleeing. It embraced
itself, hugged those corkscrew filaments, gagged

a mouth into being: the stars arranging themselves
into the figures of men, women, bears, the startled
nymphs, making patterns before eyes could see,
as it filled the newly formed air with the first scream.

THE SCATTERING

Leaving now the hired help, the niches and enclosures,
I give her ashes to the long tide
under the stars, under the wide, harsh
moonlight that kept her awake
night after night: so little gray
in such a dark sea, but finely shaded
and lighter than the air
in a tin container. I risk my skin,
though she is separated, at last,
from the rotten twine that unraveled
in her blood, knotting her brain,
closing the tiny apertures in the root
of speech. A dirge flows easily
from a battered end. The boat rocks
and hesitates and heaves on the scope
of a hand: whatever grip we move in.
I'm tilting on openness. I have something to say

about dark and fair: sister, inheritor
of someone else's anger, a crossed fate handed on;
and me, lucky, unmusical, thin as a paper clip,
keeping together. Why read catalogues,
while she dissolves toward Europe, returning
a life that almost ended on edges of glass?
The sleeping sand would absorb her history
in words. Let the sea love her,
who drowned on the second story,
where hands at the window made the arabesques
of the rhythmic dead. Her life was filled.
The body pours out. This is not herself,
though the soul crumples like paper
thrown from a boat, though voice becomes the bending
of underwater weed. Earth has a grief, trembling.
In the vacuum and total dark between the mineral
bodies of Space, a single ash whirls.

WINTER SOLSTICE

Darkest day of the year: oldest need, to lie down
in straw, in the crèche, in the welcome, dense odors
animals know their young by, where tongues wipe darkness
from eyes, the land takes cover, that white given

freely where the silver maple creaks in the wind,
the moon drifts away. Lost gifts of the Magi
clouded by sudden speech from the North, exhaustion
in the stars, nameless and opposing planets, far

suns we cannot see. Here, poinsettias settle
in us like a wound, magnificent, and winter
cactus blooms above maps of the old world, ragged
roots like torn sentences, letters of unhappy friends;

all those losses cupped in your hand opening
toward me, as pollen follows the moon like fatigue.

SCENARIOS FOR A MIXED LANDSCAPE

      Katonah Gallery: these little boxes,
lessons in order, opening; never nature, such round
      pegs, straight strips of mirror, glossy
aqua, each box a world without inhabitants, full of
      law. If my room were a box, titled
#36, listed in a browser's catalogue; if I opened
      and closed upon shifting symmetries,
with fine electric currents making invisible threads
      on the differently heated faces of a
crystal, and that crystal in my blood, moving, deathless,
      generative, indifferent as art;
if I sat outside my boxed body, its baffled corners,
      its crashing fluids, and thought my way
into a tide, into a pull behind the tongue, where
      images whirled in magnetic field, slapped
against the siding of bones: this would be one
      unrevisable event, not imitated; preceded
by words that define its limit, spasms of skin, a new self.

•

I can't conjure day lilies in front of the screen
      house, their wet orange horns
the mouths I never kiss. Each no opens its rails
      splitting toward the horizon,
as if a train would fume blackly into the hump yard,
      boxcars chattering into their
couplings, where I refuse to attach myself, or ride
      this weather out.
I grasp the genitals of daylight, I scoop
      into myself. Oh call it
mood: the special import of a lifted eyebrow,
      a curved gesture, the dressed model
naked in the painter's eye that opens fibers.
      I admire the lawn chair
in the rain, rusting in its joints, insistent.

•

Ceilings. Cats. Torn upholstery. Gas meter.
    A furniture of sawdust on the
tongue. Where is the tenant of this place?
    Eyes seal themselves shut,
lashes melt like the latest styrene capsule,
    which, swallowed, slows all
desire. We see in the darkness of a cosmic
    stomach! Ah, sister, your eyes
bulge, defy the sweep of limit, the glittering
    purview, the edge of whatever
one calls simplicity; so that falling occurs
    when the wall not there
is there. Eyelids fail. Breath fails.

•

The hand, hefting the cabbage, this head
    split from an overnight
rain, glutted with summer, hidden
    green worms: the leaf
of my hand peeling in the grasp
    of the cabbage. There must be
storms in the brain, trapped gusts
    between nerves, windy
corridors where the voice goes into
    blood, rising up, gathered
to a point, shaped with gills, spear-
    headed. The curve of Space
a huge lip? Each cell breathes, membranes
    swelling like the oxygen
bag in an operating room, each word
    the pin that traces
electrical circuits going into
    and out of sense. My hand
opens. My eyes blur, converting letters
    to numbers, my name an

equation spat out by half a hemi-
    sphere, by a gaping
and temporary metaphoric mouth.

·

Nectarine, dried out, grainy
    and sour and split
to the rough hide of the pit:
    I bite into evening's
work, standing in midsummer shale,
    a slow-moving fog,
a kind of gasping shoreline
    or strand, as if dream
split its core and the sour eye
    roamed over its dry
surfaces. A skin cleaves to the roof
    of the mouth, slackens
with speech, the left arm shuddering
    uncontrollably.
I move through a tunnel of air, swirling
    gases, into the vowel "O."
Into astonishment. Unclamping words.
    Death. Fire. The long bone
of each sentence crosswise in my throat
    blown free.

ON ELLSWORTH KELLY'S SCULPTURES

Can nature be this flat, so frontal, like a wall?
This is the plugged mouth of a tunnel, removed,
bolted to the floor, pure entrance, where body is denied.
It's the memory of ore. The blankness that darkens words.

If light could be poured like molten steel, molded
into plates that curved, held facing the sun,
and aged a thousand years, in salty air,
we'd confront it, learn to harvest wheat, with gray

at our backs. We'd lie thin and wide, heavy
with longing, our spines pulled to earth's magnetic
core. The restless among us would shift in the ground,
dig like triangles, plunge like slats, heave

like slabs over ice. We'd awaken to a slanted sky,
our mouths askew, heaviness in the right side
of our heads. Love would be a roundness dreamt
in the geometry of embrace. Hands forever horizontal.

And when they propped us in museums, the tubular
patrons, the new humanity, evolved and coinless,
would walk behind us, speaking gibberish,
as we grew sad and stiff: such chill not unhappiness,

but reduction, lost heat, where sides disappear.
They'd bring everyone on line up front, huddled
behind our faces, particular lives melding
to touch the universal surface. Anonymity the perfect art.

THE WINDOW

for Tom Killian

Gone, the old window in our kitchen door
that split the light in half, kept everything
entering the house clear only as the dust
allowed. The long green shafts and streaked petals
in stained glass are the last acts of his hands
set in our door, blazing in his high, gemmed
amaranth, the four colorless diamonds
in the center breaking the sun along
their edges, prisms casting a spectrum
divided on our hands. No saints within
these leaded borders, bodies filled with blue
each sunrise, as they bend to pious acts,
aureoles golden in the flat manner
of belief. We see more than death shifting

with the season: an abstract sun that glows
through tinctures at dusk. These round rubies flare
and hold their fire. In such warmth, art is
a shadow outside the frame of our slow
movements. We remember the man walking,
left shoulder drawn up, blood thinned by the drugs
that kept a grayness out of his gestures.
Evenings, the moon penetrates an unlit
room; the floor dissolves. No one walks through such
color in this life, upon the silvered
earth. By morning, his calyx holds our lost
imaginings; the approach of April
like his wheeled blade cutting the finest edge
that separates him from us, light from light.

THE MATERIAL CONVERSIONS

Say I arise from the present
skin of our embrace,
say I slip this form
like a spirit, though sun-drawn, still

in orbit around your voice,
our country home, August orchards,
yet simultaneous with the honking
geese homing toward the lake, and below,

green in the algaed light
among sunfish roaming the shallows:
so that as you remember white
caps and wind off Cape Hatteras,

the chill of autumn, the dry spillway
of Amawalk Dam, I will begin
unraveling toward the mist around the moon,
plunging through the slipstream, I will

turn; enter the lens of city air
through the small gaps between dioxin's
benzene ring and the chlorine
atoms of incinerated wrappers.

I will be the residue that drifts over rivers,
settling in the traffic of interiors: the song
of my return, the small kiss of my weight
nocturnal and thin as the fox-faced bat.

THE DOG

We could hear him out there past the lilacs,
all day dying beneath the Douglas fir.
His long, hound-and-mongrel body almost
flat, breath rattling in his lungs like broken
machinery, how did he manage getting
up, limping to his dish, eyes like banked fires?
Next day, the cat leaped at a low-flying
wild canary, caught that song in her jaws,
while he met us in the garage, his throat
flaccid, ears drooping, his pinched look curving
downward, sculpted into a kind of shame,
his fault, such slow death not ours to forgive.

We said nothing at dinner, mentioned no
creatures lost to us, cats with twisted
nylon string strangling the small intestine,
the white mouse buried in a parking lot,
the pheasant that flew into our screen door,
through it, and broke her neck. We thought we had
plenty of room for voiceless departures.
Each night now in dreams we hear his old man's
cough; run to the blazing pines where no sun
brings fire to sleep; feel the harsh light
leave our bones, as we enter the dark
caves of his eyes, the tunnel of his howl.

RUNNING

Up into mist before dawn, panting on the dark
road, inhaling the odors of sleep and empty
barns, the cling of hay and manure, body and breath
opening, shouldering forth, pressed into the swell

of light, my jointed luminous stripes like the bones
Halloween children wriggle at one's door, faces
masked with horror: I take the curve, brush the frosted
chrysanthemums, a cold finger probing my knee,

cords tightening in calf and ankle, I'm entering
fog, this milky air, sudden cataracts filling
my eyes, darkness dissolved from trees, I rush between
white columns, footfall echoing as if I ran

on all fours, the woods closing around me as I
race the sun, my spirit loose inside a blue skin.

ECLIPSE

> *A nothingness were we,*
> *are we, shall we always be,*
> *blooming: the nothing-,*
> *the no-one's-rose.*
>   Paul Celan

The moon is being slowly erased
by shadow; hollowed out; a thin strip
of light like a wound bleeding into pine
trees, ghastly petals of roses
trembling, as if to fall off, as if
the mockingbird trilling in the maple,
flexing his throat with whistles, chirps,
near-screams, summarized the life of birds
now disappearing from the earth,
that black sun moving into the corners
of our eyes, all vision moving to the right,
rotating, revolving around, behind us,
to the hidden side of Space: where the moon
emerges, again whitened by the light
pouring from our faces, emptying from the heart.

DISINCARNATING

I am drifting out of myself like an egg of light,
looking down on the river that souls cross, slipped
free of their garments, their soft plasma still imprinted
with faces, the twitch of lips, the look you and I

must surrender. I see the zigzag traces of their final
energies, the ribbons of speech I tried to unfurl,
wisps of darkness trailing like hair from disappearing
skulls. My hands wink out, dissolve in the star-stream.

By what sign will I know you if the spirit has no eyes?
Bands of color are jostling bones along the spectrum.
A hot spark ignites atomic air, torn spirals of molecules,
gases condensing into spines, my pale self shifting into yours.

The light I travel within begins to swell, its membrane
bursting. Am I falling within myself at such a speed,
shall I lose you to darkness? There's no voice within
cordless throats. A blunt mountain rises to meet me,

words drifting in space, seeking the shapes of mouths.
Here's where angels used to gather with their animal souls,
their goat feet, their jackal heads, their curved talons,
before beasts were driven onto the plain, pursued by fire.

GLEN ISLAND

Gulls come here to die of no visible
wound. We find them beached near the broken glass
and seawall, as if adrift, asleep, eyes
filled with sand. We've buried one with a stick

that broke halfway down, and made a crude cross.
Beyond the bay, a pile driver echoes
the pounding of our blood. What will we dream
with delicate feet folded under us?

The wheeling tern screams for the bread we toss
into the wind. And settles on Keep Off
signs. And there's the wire-mesh fence we climbed
from which we fell into ungathered leaves

like two chestnuts. We feel ourselves glowing
in this air. The breakwater divides us
from the Sound, like a crooked thumb, it marks
nothing between us. We stand here and won't

wash away. The dredging and the week's work
still to be done: a barge swaying in rust,
tugging the rope of an orange marker
where August swimmers turned against the tide.

CLOUDS

1

What is blue but absence? A cool wind. Let there be
shadows that grope on hillsides, that ripple and erase
gray mirrors in small ponds: last night's memory of lightning

the white nerve in its myelin sheath, the sprawled synapse
of the birch that cast caged shadows on the garden. Bright
days strung like beads on a single frequency, hissing by.

Let there be mornings of color: hands curling over wet cotton,
a grasp opening as cries of birds burst from the trees,
something bundling from the north, howling towards heat.

2

The empty curve: taut from horizon to horizon,
a stiff canopy. Thunder. As if the sun bowled through
a tunnel in space, and fell, and rose on white-hot wings.

Gray, driven scud: huge knees leaning on earth,
floods filling ravines, trees turgid; black billows
the fumes of flight, as sparrows crash into garage windows.

Once, these forsythia stooped under late, wet snow.
Rain gutters glistened, pulling away from the house. No
words from the ice-world. A blankness in speech like cumulus.

3

That formation of rags, caught by the wind,
fluttering over the pinched river, the gray skin of sea.
You are drawn to a salty medium, this estuary that is

the tide of our pulse, pock-marked by a needling-down
from the surface of stars, the leaking light, a turning
over: the bright sides of particles like scurf

from the moon, a kind of madness, an acid
whiteness. You open like night-blooming narcissus
to great movements, a cracking of sky, uninhabited worlds.

4

Now they are the floating heaps of bleached
dust; vistas temporary between them, where no navigation
takes us through, as if passage opened and closed, the salt

falling from the air, a swell rising beneath us, dark
seething, the hump and glow of furnaces the other side
of steel mills, low mountains. And on they drift: vast

white silhouettes, dampness and ice, the mist a soft fabric
that clings to the faces of climbers. We hear the hum
of suspension bridges, the gasp of heights, tires hot on macadam.

5

If they merged forever into a concave ceiling:
leaving us gray, etiolated, eyes useless and frosted,
fingertips the only retinas; our reach implying spaces

we have never seen; electrostatic drops warping into
the fluid wavering of gravity. Rain our inconstant
condition, gone by evening; noctilucent islands

in slow procession below the moon, dreams gaping
among trees; one's own hand translucent; shadows of stones
bulging within one's touch. A silence. Sky the only motion.

HEARING NOISES

Tinnitus. The sound of light inside my
skull, an energy-flower that opens
endless white furrows. The clatter and ping
of a struck glass, dropped silverware, sung notes,
holding. And speech flows like threads of lava
into the sea. Here is the hissing tide,
transparent bones of the grasp, drowned lovers,
hair streaming, the gurgle of the barrier
reef; a silver pulse in orbit around
the brain, the glittering rings of Saturn.

One day, surcease: a man mouthing which way
the road curves, while I hear only the rush
of rivers; keep my hand to the ground, feel
his words pounding the earth, imagine scree
in motion down the mountain, like my last
heard sentences. And deafness will begin,
spinning like ball bearings in dry sockets,
squealing. This cup, paper clip, ballpoint pen
floating free of syllables, my voice wide
in the back of my throat, breaking apart
like the squat white vase a stone falls into.

THE TOKEN

We find this smooth stone on Charlestown beach,
rubbed clean by sand tumbling in the tide,
its whiteness and share of gray the shed
skeletons of lost crustaceans, its oval eye-shape
the memory of a soft body, the wet soul that slides
free of fossilizing rock and the press of salt.

The ocean curves around us like a green lens
through which we feel the tenth planet tugging
the sky, our blood curved to its space like a red,
gibbous moon, like the stone before it died
into this blanched bone, or dried tear
of lava, this coin growing warm in my palm.

I pocket it. Behind us, the cedar-shingled homes
on stilts can take the high sea beneath them
for a little while, windows boarded against gales,
the empty carapaces of horseshoe crabs
plucked free and winging through children's dreams,
the family dog howling at the wind, a shutter banging.

WORLD WITHOUT YOU

    If this were a dream, I'd be halfway up
the Golden Chain, my ankles twisted in its links,
    angels fluttering their robes, and below
me, calloused hands of brutes, detached from wrists,
    furred and holding on. If this were a dream,
I'd break free and fall once more into the river, a depth
    of 20 feet, I'd watch the hippos cropping weeds,

I'd swim through their massive jaws. If this were a dream,
    the glossy bodies dancing in silt, the algaed
faces of lovers and suicides kissing past with closed
    eyes, I'd comb my fingers through their hair,
I'd let go sorrow like a cinder block, I'd rise to the last
    inch and film of water, to see the blue outline
of your face delicate as scrimshaw. If this were a dream,

    let loose from the river's mouth, I'd thrash
into the sea, and speak to dolphins in the helium-squeak
    of aquanauts, pronouncing your name, which even
here is flammable and quick. Bursting through the nets
    of Portuguese fishermen, limpidly finned, human
and other, quite nearly feathered, I'd fly out of this dream
    to find you.

from *Clio's Children* (1985)

DOSTOEVSKY AT SEMYONOV SQUARE, 1849

It's snowing into the prison courtyard, into the fog,
    into your sleep: bits of light chipping
    off Tatar cheekbones. They're taking you
somewhere. The young soldier, with a wispy red beard
like yours, tells you: "We have been told to tell you
    nothing." You nod. There's Petrashevksy
    and Durov, hunched shadows, temples hollow
as spoons, otherwise unchanged, like specimens in jars
of alcohol. Did they talk? The soldier reminds you of you,
    racing in the woods of Darovoye, between birch
    and hazel trees, naked swords and blue uniforms.
The wart on his cheek. A dull copper button. The beauty
of Russia, vivid as a red glove, the crushed skull
    of a horse,
    General Rostovstev's teeth: the mind sharpening itself
    on details, as hooves echo off stone walls,
you're pushed forward. Belinsky who put you here was right.
Men traffic in men. Christ wears the Tzar's epaulettes.

But who invented such cold? Thin overcoat, shirt, cravat,
    Yanovsky's borrowed suit: you're fit for an
    interview. Must you always owe 500 roubles?
"Mikhail, I shall be a great success or leap into the Neva."
"All I desire is to keep well." What is the lesson of damp
    straw? A window eight feet high? A metal
    table on which those before you etched
their names? You shiver, and recognize the silence
in the soldier's gray eyes: the five closed silhouettes
    of waiting carriages. ("Driver, to Shill's
    house. Quickly!") In you go, not alone,
four to a carriage, the one window opaque with frost.
You scratch at the light with your unbitten nail
    as the guard
    tells you to stop or he'll be flogged.

Must you be sympathetic? Poor Grigoriev
is giggling, falling apart in the corner of this last
boxed-in space you'd gladly occupy for a thousand years.

Or is this a dream, the rocking motion of a cradle?
    "Maminka, I am overcome with sadness . . ."
    The driver's whip cracking overhead like God's
knuckle, you have mother's medallion, rubbed smooth,
thumbed beyond recognition, like your first book's extravagant
    praise. A tremor in your groin.
    Father's hopes crushed in the hands
of peasants? How many ways did Belinsky do you in?
"I was wrong about D. He's a hack." You engineer
    your own interrogation, as horizontals
    invade your mind, knee jolts against knee.
At Moscow windows, you saw the patients from the Hospital
of the Poor, brushing past the hedge, their gowns open
    in the back.
    Now if some healer told you to kneel, you'd kneel.
    To go on breathing, you'd kiss
the hand opening the carriage door, as you stoop into freezing
air, gleaming cupolas above you, the Holy Virgin of Vladimir.

There must be 3000 people here, rubbing their hands,
    stamping like the soldiers' horses
    backing into dung. The steam obscuring
their eyes, the breath escaping through the peasants'
crenelated teeth, rising like the clouds above boiling
    cabbage. Your face should be wrapped in
    scarfs like bandages. You see the platform,
a bandstand covered with black cloth, under two inches
of white: the morning turning inside-out, as sun breaks through
    like a dream, like a legend
    of church spires. Oh no one will die.
How wonderful the Tzar is, his angels descending with sabers,
prodding awareness to the pitch of ecstasy. How neat they are,
    three oak posts
    in the ground, perfectly spaced. There's
    Speshnev, Palm, Mombelli, casting parallel

shadows on the snow. You're mounting the hastily built platform
outside yourself, amazed, looking down on your blond head.

Never such fatigue, never such clarity: the church
    burning through the scrim of fog,
       the sunlight like a bishop's upended crook,
glinting near your neck. You're at the far end
of the first row, intrigued by the crumpled edges
    of cloth pulled tight over angles
       and oblong shapes in the cart they're
driving up. How discreetly the driver keeps his
distance. How precisely stacked the coffins are,
    crisscrossed like fingers. Could you breathe
       on the bottom, beneath two layers of friends?
Some of you are being separated out, born noble, brought
forth: the soldier holding the sword over your head
    snaps it mid-
       air, reducing you to an ordinary man.
    Your soul writhes, convulsed, revolted
by the measure of darkness you might have unsheathed
in sour attic rooms, brandishing an axe, or hateful grin.

You kneel, disgraced and penitent, kissing
    the crucifix offered by the priest
       who walks between the rows. Your lips
almost freeze to the metal, like those of dead Jews
in a *shtetl*, face down in the ironworks, purged
    by heavenly Cossacks. Every man bends to it,
       even Petrashevsky, whom they're dressing
in a white, hooded gown, as he laughs: "They
don't know how to dress a man!" You have five minutes
    to divide three ways. Farewell to friends
       not yet tied to posts. Greetings to the worn
sinners rising like saints from the gray creases of your
brain, in the harrowing of your past, as you struggle
    to clear the
       strangled vowel of your voice in the mystery
       of being cruel to be wise. How lucky you are.
You'd have gone mad in a wallow of hopes, in a grammar
of lust, beyond the cool hand of the Tzar, uncorrected.

The last minute is for the torn lace of snowflakes
    beginning to fall; the cart horses champing
    their bits; the cupolas like domes of pale fire;
the sound of Kashkin weeping. How should this cease?
It is impossible the dead should not hear the clods
    of earth breaking two inches
    above their eyes. The rigid look
of the soldier's jaw, like the feel of your pen
draft after draft, is the first intention of a character's
    face. But whose? You would have drawn
    the great sinner, raised him above revolt,
dragged him from monasteries to gaming tables, given him
definition. Your mind is fixed on a point that trembles
    like a dust-
    mote within a drop of water
    hung by mysterious force, pulled narrow
to the flats of gravity. Your feet are suddenly heavy,
your hands wet with light. Could you rise through that sky?

Who is this galloping into the Square, waving a white
    handkerchief? You are saved. Rostovtsev
    grins. The fabled messenger has arrived
in the nick of last minutes: his moustache dryly
pasted above his lip; he is almost too late, descending
    from nowhere, his cloak hanging like
    cardboard drapery, his arms at his sides,
folded wings. Rostovtsev reads your reprieve, stuttering
through the awkward consonants you never thought to hear
    alive. But what is he announcing?
    Four years? Can the heart pronounce it?
You'll be taken to Tobolsk, to Omsk, across the salutary
waste of Siberia, deep into legendary cold, where milk
    spills in thin
    frozen slabs and despair is common as the hard
    muds of April. You do not expect to die again
in a single fetid room, hemmed in by suffering of other men
dour in brimless caps, as you invent your sin and redemption.

GEORGE SAND AT PALAISEAU, 1865

August

For the moment, no bad odor. Limbs bend. Eyes stare
      toward the memory of the hand
closing them. She washes him quickly, changes
his nightgown; plants flowers between the rim of his body
      and August air,
          faithful Alexandre.
He'd said nothing when she ran off with Marchal.
How he whimpered in the cold bath, telling her
      to continue Fuster's
          treatment, saddened
by the burden he was for Madame. Fifteen years,
still he would not use *tu*. Did she ever love a man
      not frail? His hand
          thin as light, lifting
a gesture to the window, sliding beyond her grasp.
Wheat fields, bloodied by sun, streaming toward Paris.

Without him, now, she will write . . . advice to new friends.
      Flaubert would redo the scene,
rearrange the pillows, have a cart rumble
into a rut, put the window on the west wall,
      lamplight falling obliquely
          on a youthful face.
She listens to birds. The cook's clatter. Downstairs,
last week, his sister held her ears, while he inhaled
      the *gaz*. She remembers
          Valdemosa; Chopin's pallid
hand fading into Études, while she wrote furiously,
her study a *fumoir;* workmen shaking their heads
      after hauling the piano
          up the mountain;

the smell of fish, olive oil, garlic oozing
like salt from the walls, from a thrashing sea.

She's finished the novel, *Le Bonheur*, left intact
        the bits of dialogue Alexandre
contrived. *Their* novel, to give him something
of life, in making art. She reads her diary entry:
        "The will to heal
        is all." Not the oaf
her son, Maurice, called him, he seems perfectly
quiet. He'd won some of the arguments, rewritten
        some of the parts
        for the puppet shows
at Nohant. And she sewed his clothes, the tiny
trousers, while friends argued across the room
        with the dancing
        marionettes. A son's jealousy
swells like the Indre, swirls a muddy water
about her thighs. Lovers are swept away like debris.

Men say she talks like a man, the odor of cigars
        in her hair,
clinging to her dress, the stink of equality.
What a husband forgets a son picks up as his own:
        Maurice, imminent
        landlord of Nohant, seigneur
of orchards, pavilion, and woods, telling her she's
too old. For two nights, she sits near the body,
        mourning little Nini
        and Cocoton, the grandchildren
also gone. The cupboard of her hearing about to close,
how long will she write of love? Visitors arrive, but
        not upstairs: his sister weeping,
        fearing the dead face. The church will not
bless his ground. She must carry him into plain earth.
"Do not worry. I shall not be ill. I refuse to be ill."

November

In the morning, autumn glistens. Alexandre's presence,
      as in life, recedes, allowing her
to be herself. It was good to be in Paris, the Odéon,
Théâtre-Français, where the voice carries out of Nature
      the passion life cannot
      afford. Perhaps she'll write
Marchal; tell how blood rises, old women clutch
their shawls, remembering the long hands of Liszt.
      Her mood is for children's
      tales. At night, crisp
emanations of the stars. Recently, at dawn, mist
rolling through trees, fluency returned: ten pages,
      and birds
      flapping into the wet air.
She emerges from the cloud of cigarette smoke, someone's
Muse, but does not find him etching, dark eyes dilating.

Marchal, fat darling, this morning in Paris, an early
      breakfast, someone else
in your arms, what do you remember of art?
It's a new age, seeking hardness; Flaubert's music
      of objects.
      Poor Marie, beloved Dorval,
that full voice breaking over an audience of stones.
"Dear Gustave, what are you doing?—grinding away,
      I fancy, you, in solitude too . . .
      mother probably in Rouen. Do you
sometimes spare a thought for 'the old troubadour
of the ale-house clock, who sings, and will always sing
      of perfect love'?"
      The wind creaks toward winter,
sweeping voices aloft, an opera of the damned. Someone will
write of her. The peasants of La Châtre? A drunken mayor?

No one believes in her minor aches—as if she owned
      more than her reputation,

with Solange, her daughter, the slut of Europe!
The lead weight of the Second Empire still keeps wives
      in place. Let the lovers
      enter their fiacres,
drive south away from husbands who tattle in books
about nothing. In old age, a new magnetism: the moon
      drawing up the vapors
      of a ragged field,
pulling at her blood, tugging the half-surfaced soul
that keeps going under. In abstinence, a red death.
      Marchal, huge springtime,
      we grow plump, and France
lacks exaltation. How many dinners purchase a hug?
I'm an infant, without sex or energy, blinking at the dark.

She pulls at her hair, remembering how she'd cut it off
      and sent it in a box
to Musset, a final blow. Poor Alfred, on the crossing
to Genoa, groaning in his cabin, sick as a girl.
      She wrote for hours,
      stood on deck, took sea-spray
full in the eyes. Delacroix would paint her now
all lines, without color: changing his art
      because she did not
      remain young.
She can still look to heaven! Hands clasped, face
pale in its own light. She can still hear Balzac
      huffing up the stairs,
      hugging loaves of bread
for Jules and the runaway Aurore. She hears mice. A faint
scratching at her heart. Things from God that must return.

WILLIAM MORRIS BOATING UP THE THAMES TO KELMSCOTT MANOR, 1880

You name this rented houseboat
The Ark, going upriver, through locks and weirs,
where men pile August hay on punts, the corn-crake cries in grasslands,
rooks scream in elms. That's the odor of lime. It's almost a day
    to forget the unemployed, police batons,
    sooty faces; sun setting this water ablaze,
while retired colonels, reading the *Times*, hoot from armchairs, praise
horses riding into uplifted hands. Jane's in the cabin, fighting off
    asthma: the black fog in her lungs, your
    proximity. She never enjoyed a broad body,
woodworker's hands. Long and pallid, Rossetti's dream in blue
silk: she's full-length, free now of pain in her back; black hair
    descending in waves, hands folded, Dante's
    wife jailed above the marshes of Maremma.
You, and daughters, and friends, towed by Biffen's men: goggle-eyed
drunk; another, too thin. They hook you onto a mercantile tin kettle,
    your bow slapping all the way to
    Twickenham, spray in your beard.

    Tea above Kingston: color
    imprinted like fingers burning through
the sky; your mind streaked by Northern Lights, twisting
toward Thorshaven, crags of Iceland, wasted slopes, the happiest
    struggle in the face of death. Jane pours.
    DeMorgan calls you an imposter. You get another
tow, after dismissing Biffen's men. You haven't touched an oar yet.
The girls clap. You'll cook for everyone! Men should live with plain
    floors, whitewashed walls. Oh let them
    scrape Oxford smooth, obliterate a rough-hewn
joy. No future's clean. Jane tucks away the letters from Rossetti,
words heavier than that barge of bricks; hands cool. Oh you'll cook!
    In Moulsey Lock, waiting for the water
    to raise *The Ark*, gates to swing open,

you drop the candle from the lamp, a spring slips, light hisses out.
"By damn!" Jane blinks. Here, there's no window to throw dinner
      out of. You won't
         kick a rented door into the Thames.

         You and Price sleep in *The Ark*,
      the hot night, swaying. The ladies and Dick
and DeMorgan hold their noses at the Magpie Inn, try the foul
beds. You listen to toads and crickets. The boat, rising
      on the tide's inhalations, begins to move
         away from the mooring, away from the simple
loops of quick hands. (You know where this water flows: river
before the maelstrom epileptics dream of, falling off to nowhere.
      Jenny's twitching in her bed, frail
         daughter.) How beautiful she was, Jane
in repose, your Guenevere; the cup you brought her, a muted gleaming,
as in tapestries the wealthy pay you to hang on their walls. What
      does man leave but the memory of
         labor? It's morning: sky fleeing westward,
your line in the water. One gudgeon. A small dace. They gasp
in your world. You watch the knot of swallows overhead, in pursuit,
      opening like a bag of needles above the hawk,
         chasing him toward Eaton Hastings.

         Everyone's back on board by 10:00.
         Another lock. A long tow to Windsor Bridge.
The day effortless and languid as the look of Burne-Jones's
women, though you bark your shins, wasps find you hove to.
      The air quick, whimsical, you're in the cabin,
         cooking on the spirit-lamp, DeMorgan outside,
swatting. The girls run along the bank, falling into high grass.
(No savage workers here, blackened faces rising like apparitions
      in northern smoke.) Sunset!
         Even Jane laughs, going ashore, buttoning
the top of her dress, while haze settles on the river's throat.
Good lodging at Bridge Hotel: beds clean, empty as space in warps;
      the women in one room, giggling;
      the men here, snoring like Biffen's drunk.

(At Hammersmith, upstairs, you wanted only reasonable labor,
reasonable rest: solace of the loom at dawn, rattling the shuttle
      back and forth; Jane under the covers,
    stopping her ears, while you shook the room

        with patterns of daisy, wild grape,
    papered the walls with vegetables, fruit, above a street's
torn cry, unmended lung.) You can't sleep in such noise, thinking
of Iceland's hummocks. Lava fields. Nakedness of glaciers, massive
      capes slipping from bony
    shoulders; all that white collapsing in sun,
into Rossetti's hands. You stare at the wall's scarlet flock;
flowers fading in dampness. DeMorgan's on his back, stertorous,
      shattering the air; the river hidden;
    not even merlins flying in thick mist,
your eyes wet, fingers itching. There's no tool to shape this mood.
A good day to see Eton! You buy bread, and Price discovers
      a cucumber thick as a boy's
    arm. You're fine, afloat, until Bray Lock:
your foot throbs, goutish, tender, as if gripped too long; Jane's
wincing, blood rushing from her face into the twisting of her
      spine. DeMorgan shouts.
    Too late. *The Ark* drifts into a pair of barges,

      the starboard door splinters
    like a thin wall. You can smell the cargo
of green timber. Price falls into a mock faint. You trade
epithets with the captain, steer off, shaking your fist. May
      writes in your diary:
    "a mountain before a plain . . .
a dust heap before a gentleman's house." At last, chalk
slopes falling away, past Cookham. You've avoided another
      tin kettle. (Is there a way to change
    course? You decorate palace walls. Empire swells
to engulf Afghanistan, for a "scientific frontier," lashes out
at Kaffirs, the Zulus. Gladstone's homily is of tragic ends. No
      use in your painted thistle.)
    Tonight, you sleep in *The Ark*,

on the flood, while Jane curls up at the Inn. Aurora Borealis:
light splits open; the moon dissolves. In Iceland, nothing so green
>   as this day, or quick
>   as the silvery bleak huddled at your line.

>   Next morning, it's Lady Place
>   and Margrave. The women watch two men
splashing naked in the river. "They're looking for Moses
in the rushes." Even Jane titters. Suddenly, there's a line
>   of poor children at water's edge
>   whining, begging for coppers. Anger
explodes in your hand waving them away. You damn the accident
of birth that put them there; you, here. But you reach Oxford:
>   Salter's mooring. Charles will meet everyone
>   at Radcot, lifting the lantern as you disembark,
voices drifting toward the shadows of polled trees. High up and safe
at Kelmscott, Jane will open Rossetti's letters. You'll sigh,
>   solicitous about his health; she'll lie down beneath
>   his drawings from Dante, another headache coming on.
Is that a blue titmouse? They've not returned with weed sparrows,
pigeon hawks, rooks filling the trees. There's a moorhen; a Cotswald
>   look to that house, before they blind
>   the birds with zinc roofs. You have things to do!

>   Books to open. A worker unfolds
>   his fabrics, lifts swollen hands from the vat
like a drone made beautiful by indigo. Charles swings the lantern,
laughs. Women tumble onto the dock, dresses wet along the hem,
>   your hands hardened by rope and oar,
>   face a deeper red, hair wild. You open the door
in the garden wall. It's home: tapestries, stony spaces between;
stairs twisting in the grain of oak trees, split to a knot; leaded
>   windows not rattling to heavy feet.
>   Jane's lying down. The girls are yawning.
You can't sit still. Rossetti shivered here, complained of dampness
from the Thames, Jane brushing her hair, while you talked of Burne-
>   Jones: problems of painting women,
>   downcast eyes, profit in craft.

You'll limn no more nymph or faun, lurid leaps across a lord's
cabinet; Jane sitting up, pale, a sculpted Echo. Upriver, you hear
   workers cough blood in shadows of iron
      railings, see the sun fail in dusty gardens.

EMMA GOLDMAN DEPORTED TO RUSSIA, 1919

Even on Ellis Island, they split darkness before dawn:
    key scraping in the lock; two guards.
"Get ready." Ethel drops everything, trying to stuff clothes
into a bag. Can such girls be enemies of the state? The male
    deportees huddle in the corridor, one on crutches,
    another carried from his bed, ulcer bleeding
quietly. Berkman, your Sasha, is counting men into groups, arranging
for last telegrams, telephone calls. The inspectors
    say there will be time. But there isn't.
    A brooch holds together the top of your dress,
like a butterfly trapping warmth. You walk between the railings
of the Reception Center, the high wall, where wives from Poland
    lined up for physicals, eyelids lifted
    for signs of trachoma, sick ones marked on the sleeve
with chalk. Palmer and Hoover, physicians of the state, oh they've
x'd you here, winter's coat too short, one's soul showing through
    like a long wrist. The wind rattles windows
    in four towers, howls through arches, stirring snow

into a mist, moonlight glancing off the brooch into the eyes
    of officials. Can they see sedition
inside tin trunks? A thin deportee is weeping, pulling
his portmanteau, avoiding feet. The man in extra coats
    cannot bend to snatch the orange
    rolling across the floor.
"Line up!" It's Caminetti, his uniformed boys. Outside,
deep whiteness; wind almost breaking your grip; armed men
    lining the way, tight-lipped and gray
    as the barge at anchor, that shadow heaving
toward the skyline you cannot see. Are you leaving for Hades?
Grunts. Threats of beatings. A man pushed to the frozen dock.
    Someone blows a whistle all the way
    to Bedloe's Island, and women cross the gangplank,

no heavy coats trailing. Ethel's pulling away from the young
soldier, your footsteps firm, resounding, as he calls after her,
 "I'm sorry!" You hear Sasha telling men
 to keep their bundles taut, hide their money.

The cabin thick with heat; iron stove crackling its innards
 like nutshells. No water. No air. The city
in the porthole, shrinking: Thirteenth Street, Union Square,
half your friends put away. The opaque film evaporates from your
 glasses; sweat trickling into the folds
 of your neck; stains spreading like an eclipse
under each arm. The girls shake free their hair, all this wonder
you once had; full bosom; the high lyric of your voice broken
 by nightsticks. What did you accomplish,
 passing beneath the torch of that woman,
her eyes bleeding toward the sea? You feel the world wobble
on its axis. You hear Sasha arguing. Everyone's buttoning up.
 You're outside, climbing stairs up a rusted
 wall, the decrepit *Buford*, an old troop ship.
The men go into steerage, already cold. No doctor says, "Cough."
Metal bunks. Straw mattresses. Two basins to vomit in. That's
 Hoover in the launch, yelling,
 "Merry Christmas!" You thumb your nose.

You sleep all day. No vigilantes rush into your cabin,
 twisting the testicles of lovers. No dreams
of auditoriums, your cheeks flushed, men in the front row,
looking up, gleaming like wet stones. Why is this room damp?
 The ground without trees? You stumble to the door.
 He's young enough to bow, the soldier
grabbing your arm, following you to the toilet. Twelve hours?
You're that far away from yourself, New York, decency. You demand
 to talk with the men. "Impossible." But Sasha's
 let up, to tell you about thin blankets, leaky
bulkheads, salt water for washing, the lack of soap, threadbare
towels. The guards think you shot McKinley. Bombed the local
 church. Sasha bends over with cramps,
 stiffens in his steps, while they ask you about

dynamite, anarchist crimes. Now your men are singing old songs,
in a language that hardens beyond recall, that congeals the tongue,
    breaking off like taffy.
    Where will you not be a stranger?

January. The English Channel. An Allied destroyer in your narrow
    wake. There's no bread, before the North Sea,
drifting and forgotten mines. Badly listing, you slip through
the Kiel Canal; stop for repairs. Men locked below are crumpling
    notes for the German workers, tossing out
    news, while sledges thunder on the hull.
Welders pull away in boats, singing of revolution. *Matushka Rossiya!*
You, Red Emma, can't remember the Russian for "bowl," "pencil,"
    "breast." Have you reversed the tilt of your
    womb? Lovers left you for children; left you
on platforms, sweating, as police roared up the aisles, clubbing
words back into mouths, shackling men who would not go to war.
    Now the *Buford* can't dock at Libau.
    The White Army's fighting to the death; the Baltic
crowded with blood, blockade, intervention. The engine pounds.
Shudders. Halts. You hear the flat, feverish cries of men
    with daughters in Chicago, their frozen
    breath shattered in midair.

Finland. Safety. At Hango, you get provisions to live on
    three days. Bayonets poke you
toward the train, soldiers open your packages, bundles, helping
themselves to scarfs and cheese. Sasha lines up the men,
    dear friend, even here, at blocked
    exits, he finds air at the hinge of every
door. The Americans, their ship, the young soldiers, fade
like wind-blown fog over miles of ice, a thickened harbor
    closing behind them. A stern lieutenant
    says, "Speeches will not do here." In what
idiom do you answer? You can barely speak, after thirty-five
years: government's paunchy, red-eyed jailers; the matrons who cut
    your ration; clerks with ink-stained fingers
    tucking money under blotters, pointing always

to the curve of sky, where light disappears. You send telegrams
to the People's Commissars. Wrench a last scarf out of dirty hands.
    Soon you'll be home. There'll be Feinberg.
    Gorki's wife. Kisses that do not penetrate.

Workers and peasants surround you at the border: eyes glowing
    in dark recesses. Music. Song. You are welcome
here, the American felon, the daughter returned, weeping
on the road to Petrograd. Sasha's sick; solitude breaking loose
    in his lungs. Zorin takes you
    in his car through quiet streets, the snow clean
in headlights. Sudden forms. Bright circles in the eyes. Hands.
"*Propusk!*" Zorin produces his pass. Rifles wave him on. Was there
    a revolution? You stay in the Astoria Hotel;
    others in the Smolny, school for aristocrats.
Zorin's wife, pregnant, lays out herring and kasha, moving in and out
of shadow, tall against the larder. She talks of hunger, created
    by the compassionate West. The old guard's armies
    that scar Russia; Denikin, Kolchak, Yudenich
spilling blood of new-born consciousness. Strong backs needed now.
Harsh ways. Glittering squads at dawn. Trunks filled with *propuski*.
    No one worse than your own intelligentsia.
    Sasha keeps asking: "Who is this 'it'?"

Days of talk. Old friends, like Bill Shatoff, bulging in the cold
    with open arms. At the anarchists' meeting,
you hear of the Cheka. Machine guns. Bolsheviks seizing food
and fuel. Not everyone speaks at the Petro-Soviet. Long queues
    for wormy cereal, frozen potatoes,
    bloated blue prostitutes tugging the sleeves
of Red soldiers. It's the blockade, Zorin says. Counterrevolution.
The flabby Zinoviev agrees, his voice cracking like an adolescent's.
    You nurse Sasha, break his fever; speak
    soothingly into the night. Zorin's wife
laughs at the offer of infant clothes. You, pampered *bourgeoisie*,
remember how Papa beat you in Königsberg. Now, the Party rules
    with *rastrellyat*, bullet-chipped walls. The people
    are stupid. Dark. Brutal. One beats them back,

Lenin's wolf at their throats. Only the indignant labels change,
like *Defiance,* the clothes you made in prison, listening to Missouri
   accents. Night-sounds. Rumbling trucks. You
     pull the covers to Sasha's chin, shivering yourself.

BRUNO BETTELHEIM AT DACHAU, 1938

Run. Run. Inside the Jourhaus, they erase your name.
        The nearest face blurs
           into a voice, shrieking
you cannot replace your broken glasses here.
You can't see the sleeve of the new man you are.
        In the distance of rattling
           cattle cars, a sudden engine
takes away your breath, grizzled men sneer.
A tyro, your number is too high. They tell you
        about the old days,
           when the smart ones died.
Ten miles from Munich? Earth's end seemed further
toward darkness, the edge of a Polar sea, beyond
        habitation. Your head aches.
        You're bleeding from your
side. If you faint, they will carry you off,
into the space between trees, their final empire.

The guard tells you to pick up the pebble,
        bring it
           rolling to his palm.
It's the wrong one. Older prisoners stare at dirt
lodged under fingernails. If the rifle butt comes
        down, you'll never again
           tie a string: child, fumbling
with shoelaces, despised like the man eating grass,
"Moslem" in filth. Will another pebble change you?
        Will there be a Bettelheim
           using "I,"
awakening in a different skin, rushing out at 4 a.m.,
when sirens scream for the peeling away of self?
        He laughs, walking away,
        only a boy

talking of your castration. In prison, a man
spits on his neighbor, reviles his God, slaps his friend.

Here's the Kapo. Jew beating Jew. You face the wall
      like a dunce, you become
      invisible. You can't ask the enemy
why he assists the enemy. You quiz a failing memory:
name the town you come from, the school, who wrote
      the last letter,
      quoting someone who quoted
you. There's a middle-class man weeping
because they do not call him *Herr*. Is there
      status on the dung
      hill? The SS marches
through, where frail men stare at stones
like autistic children. Others are waving flags,
      tightening armbands,
      jealous brothers
complaining to father. You walk, to find out
what a man's born to be, curving to the shape of a blow.

Three weeks. Not three years. You're still alive.
      The guard shoots
      over the row of straw beds.
Nothing nicked. It's a good job. You can get on line
for coffee. In winter, they let you sleep
      until the farm animals
      yawn, and stir,
standing in stalls, stained by their own urine.
Are they driven out five abreast? The guard is pointing
      to your number.
      He's taking you
to the Jourhaus, for release, smiling. Finally,
you've been recognized, paid for, lifted dripping
      from a sewer. But he brings you
      back. Oh some mistake
on your part, having hope. A truncheon prods body
to the limit. The spirit snaps like a small stick.

Starvation edema. Cheeks swollen. Eyes glittering.
     The orchestra of ragged men
     had brass violins
in your dream. And he's done it, the man
who promised to hang himself. How does one hold on?
     You'll always sleep
     curled into a ball.
This one clutches a crust of bread. He calls women,
and whimpers, and masturbates, with no result.
     There's nothing special
     about dying. Why do the new ones
talk of escape? The Kapo ladles soup from the top
if you're stupid. Your blood's thin as an old woman's,
     whispering in your ears,
     the mind a bowl
filling with images. You lift something to the light
like the rumor of a double ration of bread. An idea.

Record. Remember. It's what the child you took into your
     home could not feel
     in his clenched fist.
He arrived without a name to turn to, almost without
a skin, a surface to touch. You taught him textures
     of food, the point of a pin,
     the arc of an encircling arm.
Did he remain numb to spite your goodness? When
does the tongue taste sand? Only new prisoners talk
     of humiliation. War.
     Think, rather, what vegetable's
in the soup. How the guard knocks men with glasses
into the latrine pit, calling them "asshole,"
     while the Brick Commando
     trots past. How the Commandant,
impersonal as a photograph, standing in the compound
back of his home, peers through a hole in your chest.

EUGENE O'NEILL AT TAO HOUSE, 1941

He wakes sweating from a dream of fog.
It's here: the cough, the rattle of the lunger, flophouse
salute; something lone gone in the kidneys. Ship's bells.
      Yesterday, words spiraled
   across the page, out of reach, his hands
trembling. In his study, in the porthole light, it's 1912:
a lost tide washing down blank paper like watered whiskey.
      He'll shrive them all:
   mother, dazed as ever, gesturing
like St. Francis at birds never there. He hears
Jamie's greeting from the clipped shrub, the woody thing
   that grows even in death, his brother
grinning; sweat pouring from wastrel's chin into collarless
shirt. Their words begin to blur. Black out. Like the bulbs
   father said, burning, would put him in the poorhouse.
The last play? Whatever flame he sinks into now, from which he
   came, burns away the voice, consumes cathedrals.

Each day's silence, like the war, a thin
cloud settling on walnut trees; sun disappearing into
long grasses on Mount Diablo. Carlotta's hidden the house
   in its white walls;
   "Keep Out" signs blocking the mile-long
road; wrought iron twisted on the gate, ancient symbols
spelling out "The Way." She types scenario, dialogue,
   using her magnifier,
   his script so small it's almost flattened
to her palm; still the actress she was in photos, posing
in the Grecian manner, head against his cheek, both of them
   facing a distant sky, the shrinking
gods. How he misses the sea. It's easy to navigate dry
between colored mirrors, teakwood dragons, Chinese Chippendale,
   Coromandel screen; everything from
Gump's edge of the world, an hour's drive, the city intact.
   Shop windows crackling in the moon's wake.

Like Hickey in Hope's saloon, he bullies
dreaming spirits to drive them out of doors, keeps dropping
the pencil. Coffee spills on his sleeve, brown swill, words
　　　　　　sinking beneath unsteady
　　hands, like the keys of a player piano.
"You should have nothing else to do," Carlotta says. "Just
write." And closes the blinds, her eyes in pain from sunlight,
　　　　　　too used to the semidark.
　　　Shane's coming for a visit, the son
draining him like alimony, who wants to raise horses in Colorado.
"Let him scrub decks on a ship. My father kept me on the dole."
　　　That night, his legs twitch, he tries to run,
and wakes, remembering the house on Peaked Hill Bar sliding
into the sea. Do parents ever love more than themselves? Sudden
　　　　　wind in the valley. Who'll feed him, when the spoon
falls? At Jimmy the Priest's, he rose from the cot like Lazarus,
　　　　　vomiting Veronal and five-cent whiskey.

　　　He's weak, following the brick path in back
that winds upon itself; standing in the new pool, looking
over the tiles, down the mountain. There's Blemie, his old
　　　　　Dalmatian, taking the sun,
chipmunks tearing across the lawn, Carlotta
pink against the peach groves, fidgeting with her blouse
and hair, hands suited to music, contemptuous as glass.
　　　　All writing washed away
　　at Dunkirk: gone, the world's drowse; gone,
the road to Le Plessis, rented chateau, where his Electra
listened to her ghosts. Everything sinks far away. Poland.
　　　Finland. France. Radio news: his silence.
This, too, is history, a man speaking into his private dark.
In the core of his bones, a tremor; knees knocking; the earth
　　　　heaved up in fire. The British are mining
the sea lanes of Singapore, while Carlotta waves, Blemie struggles
　　　to his feet; not even clouds darken the valley.

from *Walking Four Ways in the Wind* (1979)

CREEDMOOR: THE LOCKED WARD

I ask what she needs
write it down
she can't
her penmanship's
a five-year-old's
hair cut close to her head

        mother wants a boy
        and who doesn't

weeping into a balled-up tissue
next time bring tissues
and shoes
would I buy brown shoes?

        tell mother to call
        where is mother
        tell mother to forget it

two fat women
in the immense dayroom
waltzing arm in arm
the boy who borrows cigarettes
        behind them
        singing a hymn

I can't buy shoes
without her feet

        she'd give me
        her feet

I'm thinking of my wife and daughter
I want to leave

        bring tissues

between the casement windows
the young woman laments
   her abortion at 20
   who really had none

   what happened to the dog
   did you put him to sleep
   where is mother?

I look across the room
at the unused pool table
cues lined up dusty as WWI rifles

   small voices weeping
   in my throat

smell cooking smell
canned peas and carrots
Salisbury steak

   thin gravy voice
   of the old schoolteacher
   playing old songs
   at the piano

   the fat women
   trotting in a circle

   the boy with crinkled knees
   saying his doctor
   will never change

   asks me for a nickel
   asks me for a pencil

O it's time
traffic is heavy
the bridge tolls up
I live across two rivers

I've filled her shopping bag
full of Kools
cookies soft candies
a new robe

        love to the family
        don't forget love to the family

THE KNUCKLER

We knew your stooped figure in Astoria Park,
knuckle-baller, your hand slow & disdainful
on the diamond beneath the TriBoro Bridge,
fingers forking behind your back. Whatever you
threw wobbled in the air like a soap bubble.
Your mother was the nicest woman in a yard
full of cukes & tomatoes. She bought you aquariums,
little oxygen pumps, a Schwinn, blowups of father.
She thought you too thin. She bought you huge
mittens, big-shoulder coats, while the McDonald
brothers spit on the metal doors of grocery cellars
where you slipped. Anyone at all could find
you in Mendel's, at the magazine rack, slipping
girlies between the pages of *Sports Illustrated*.

All those years, you waited for a fast sign:
a wave from the blonde divorcee in her bedroom
across the driveway. Through Woolworth binoculars,
webbing of blinds, you learned the moles & fine
track of her spine, the rayon slide of her buttocks:
her hands behind her back unhooking a fullness
in your head, behind your eyes, in your throwing hand
that had only a knuckler, only an odd way of holding on.
We couldn't hit you at all in those days,
the gray & muggy afternoons when the ball should
have carried into the East River. We popped up,
we grounded out, the boys from Seymour's Hardware,
& Baker's Garage, & Queeco's Beer, we whiffed in
sunlight, or under cumulus, in the shadow of a long bridge.

But she died suddenly, thirty-eight, a bad heart:
released from your grip, writhing in a midnight glare.
It was obviously your fault. You stopped going
to Mendel's. Sold your Schwinn. Gave up fishing
for minnows in the bay near La Guardia: that airport
built on garbage, carriage wheels, father's shoes.

You stopped catching killies in bent window-screens,
stopped bringing them home alive in tomato cans,
& pouring them into the tank with your tropical fish,
like common children among angels, while your guppies
with the bulbous eyes gave birth & ate their young
beneath the 25¢ pink plaster bridges. You took apart
the pumps. You began to focus on empty windows, sparrows.
All morning, all afternoon, we hit you, O we hit you.

WIDOW

It happens in ways I never expect,
like hailstones in summer. Going
uphill on the bike, I snap the chain.
In the tub, shaving my legs, I cut
my throat on my ankle. I sweat nightly,
pull back the blankets, see my
husband just lying down in the mirror.
I burn my hand on the iron
I test with spit: the children tumble
in from the yard with a dead bird.
I pretend, alone. I cook
for pale guests seen only at 10 p.m.
They forget to wipe their mouths,
chattering like starlings. I bang
the table and they disappear, black
coffee spilled on the white tablecloth.
I've given up smoking, I try push-ups;
for lungs and double chin, I stand
on my head: watching the late news,
the bombs falling up the sky, the men
ascending in their bloody uniforms.

SIBLINGS

When the body
is an empty suit in the closet
I whisper I am
and know that I will not be

and when I am not
anywhere to be seen or heard
will my last thought
become the first cry
of a baby girl in Peru
born and held in the web of my death

as I too was born
of an English coal miner
gasping his life into the chain
through me
in the links of flowers
grown from rotted mouths

My sister
you will leave the locked room
your deaf madness
our father's terrified soul
the dark bird
will fly out of your mind
to become a condor in the Andes

a lizard breaking birds' eggs
yolks dripping from his jaws

RELEASE

1

Sunday, in my office,
opposite the beige brick church,
I look up from the blank page.
The four clocks in the four faces
of the tower are telling different
times. Each way I turn,
the hands of the separate clocks
of the separate selves
pose into this and that
posture, dancers
test and change their gestures,
turning four faces one by one
to me, each face that I fear
to become or to come out of.

2

There I am
in the photo
wearing a sawtooth beanie,
throwing a pink rubber ball at the camera:
1945, the fleet's coming up the Hudson,
barooming salutes. The Pom . . . Pom . . . Pom
is not the noise I expected,
not ripping the air.
I throw the ball at the camera
which is being held by Mr. Weber
home from Italy with a wooden leg.

Profile: boy with hooked nose,
hair curved over forehead and behind ear;
silver jacket with fur collar.
Some mistake of the film.

Strange exposure.
The boy stares
at something beyond the frame.

Is that me, fat and blond,
held up in my father's arms?
I clutch the lapel of his pin-stripe suit
while the roof's
black tar and open chimneys
devour the sunlight.

Alice poses on the roof,
my sister: just plump enough
to swell out beneath
the edges of her bathing suit.
TV antennas poke at the sky like broken claws.
Her English jaw hangs heavy on her smile.

We're sitting in the bright sun
of Uncle Charlie's backyard
near the el's spiderweb shadows.
In short pants,
propping Danny on my lap,
I scowl at the camera
and wonder why brothers cry all night.
His pug nose defies
definition.

Nowhere do I find my mother
married. Another roof picture:
almost seven years before
her daughter will be born.
She's 20: her white dress
stark against the black roofs and open doorways.
The turn in her eye is coy,
evading the camera's eye.
The frills on her short sleeves are pretty.
The Depression is still on.

There I am
on the beach
holding my brother Stevie.
He squints at the sun and reflects
the scowl of my father,
who is propped on his elbows in the sand.

Sometimes they all seem dead
though they try to pursue me into marriage
and my thirty-fifth year and though I often
wake with my father in my arms trying to save him
from his early death and I still cannot find
a picture of my mother married and the coy eye
evades me in my dreams and my sister grins on the roof.

3

Instructor of English, appointed 1967
(smiling)

No, this can't be right

Mr. Allman shines white on black
on the door of 205 Eddy Hall

a trapped hawk claws
the back of my eyes

I walk on naked feet
from one abstraction into
another   coughing up feathery bones

    diplomas curl on the wall
Married,
one child, daughter, age six

4

For Eva whom I describe
as the nymph leaping out of the summer night
into my room:

why should I mark you with words
like savage tattoos?

The Jerome Avenue el squeals
in the valley beneath us
sparking the midnight
our veins thunder   they thunder
love's release

all night
the hollow-eyed white bird
calls
my love
my love
damn these words
what are words
what are words
rags stuffed into a mouth

it seems so long ago
we married

5

The future holds her in a box,
a small woman with hair turning white.
Even in death, her eye turns away.

The mad don't get madder
biting the spoons in their mouths
(tranquilizers steam in the blood
like fog on a tropical river, the air
fills with the cries of beautiful birds).

The clocks on the four faces of a tower
turn their sibling hours into lust,
meditation, fear, and a blank face:
the nothing that fills in each minute
like a sound that congeals in the air,
a noise that is seen, suddenly, twisting
into a vapor, a thread, that passes away.

6

I awaken to the midnight bird
who ruffles his wings, preening
(no humans in my dream,
only the sun here, the bird).
On the tips of my fingers
there are tiny photographs
and my eyes open their lenses
to let something fly out
fluttering toward carnival mirror
camera close-ups: gyrating faces,
big noses, small eyes, rectangular mouths.
Sudden silence. The sun's myriad
bells toll out light
that beams upward from my cool sheets,
my wife's hips. I arise spreading my arms
like a frail bird running into a thin breeze,
I'm aloft, above the glinting Hudson River,
riding upwards on a voice I still cannot hear,
impelled on its beautiful pure lung force,
up, up, up, my brain softly exploding,
fingers stroking my head, my eyes,
my beak. There is wreckage everywhere
washed up on the mud islands, where the sun's knives
cut through water: beer cans, twisted logs, scummy
weeds, curled strips of exposed film. I see the
body of a dog and I scream for joy.

7

The face appears on the blank page:
my mother's eyes;
the nose hooked like her mother's.
The jaw belongs to some Victorian
Englishman, or a coal miner
who looks like D. H. Lawrence.
It's me.

The Methodist Church
turns a paler beige year by year.
The rectangular tower
keeping four points of time
turns in a circle
and hands on the clocks
give their gestures
in the repetition of hours.

I hear the fleet coming downriver
in fog, barooming salutes,
while the tall boats, draped in black,
carry the dead to sea.

THE SOUL PLAYS YOU BET YOUR LIFE

But I'm the famous one, wiggling
my eyebrows, tapping my cigar,
asking her what question would
she stake all on, what category
good at: Flowers of Tibet?
Diseases of New Jersey?
She's coy, edging away, unmarried.
Never had what you call a job.
Dates older men with bad hearts
and insurance. I can't believe it,
lovely thing like her (want something
on the side, eh? rolling my eyes).
She likes movies with a message,
strawberry malts that foam over.
Her half sister was the quadroon
with bleached hair, in black undies,
who took up in New Orleans with
unnamed politicians. She herself
at twelve was had by an uncle,
at thirteen by an aunt. Later,
in two-piece Jantzen, sequin shoes,
she was Miss Used Car of Tupelo.
She knows the songs from old musicals,
does a little dance, does her imitation
waltz and call of the Depressed Canary.
I'm flipping the white cards of her
categories, her fears, her memories
of cities with rivers, high winds,
bridges that fell, the worst tornados.
She looks pale as a first-nighter
dreaming of broken legs and the hook.
I come at her suddenly bristling:
a booking agent with impatient
moustache. My top question is worth

a two-week cruise on the *Eastern Star*
that never enters the 12-mile limit.
All the Black Jack and Craps
she can handle, all the gigolos
from here to Rio, Big Bands,
top singers, unlimited cash.
The smoke from my cigar settles
around us like a fog, as I tell her
I'm the consolation prize.

THE SOUL GROWN LAZY

Dressed in black &
overweight, her voice damp:
she sighs, telling me of father
off on a big job overseas,
papa & his brothers.
I'm showing her the night city,
frowsy shops in alleys.
Little boys pick my pockets
& signs hang in windows
of restaurants: Credit Good.
No aunts behind us,
no Registrar, no mayor dozing
beneath a floppy hat, just
her loneliness, huge & flabby,
leaning against me.
I feel sweet. I kiss
the fourth fold of her neck,
my hand travels the ring
of her waist, I find
the many paths to her breasts.
She's worrying: what if we're
caught what if the police
come screaming red-faced
into the alley what if
she's really no good eating
pizza & doughnuts drinking
vanilla malts watching
TV all day sleeping waking
up eating the blankets filling
the tub with ice cream her
lips always caked with
chocolate frosting will I
love her will I love her?

THE SOUL WALKS OUT

His fever up to 103, while she quoted others:
her walking out now just wasn't right.
Such thin histrionics, the way she dropped
her box of beauty marks, leaving stars everywhere;
counting out unused Pokerino coupons, kissing
the prize velvet dog. Hadn't it been a good time?
But she didn't care: suitcase crammed with hard
times, hard candies, fake eyelashes, her Gideon.
So he'd seen the secret moles on her back, plucked
one true souvenir hair and taped it on his wall.
Was that so much? Listen, he was no saint.
He was going to sleep, sick, air-conditioning high.
She just better not be here when he woke up.

SURGERY

The dwarf nurse takes my temperature.
There's a pencil in my mouth. Already,
I'm eating my words, when she turns
to my five-year-old daughter dressed
in white curtains like a bride. It
doesn't matter, she's the doctor: here's
my new jellybean heart stuffed in a
thimble. I'm the cat mewing in doll's
clothes, ready to die, and she blows
into the thimble to bring my heart alive,
tells me I can't move, only babies cry.
I'm in surgery on the bathroom floor.
The green light darkens on the wall.
Am I in Bellevue? The medication trays
rattle in the hallway. Tug whistles
are moaning on the river like old women.
The dwarf nurse winks. She adjusts her
brassiere. My daughter is counting her
fingers. A gong sounds. "Calling Dr. No."
What have I denied? I'm marked with
lipstick, sticky X, and spit. Physician
with my wife's brow, my brother's grin,
she's digging in, unclasping my sternum.
I'm an open ship's hold taking cargo of
turtle hearts and she's lowering
her thimble on a thread into the hold
closing slowly as a cat's iris.
Someone is flushing a toilet.
The nurse sprinkles sugar on my stomach.
A cat rushes up and licks it off.
Everyone nods. The PA system plays the wedding march.
My daughter puts a monocle over the open wound,
slips skin around the edges of a glass hole.
I'm finished. I lift my head and see into it.
I can look into the picture-window egg of my soul
where snow falls forever on the tiny house.

A FORMER LIFE

A narrow cobbled street:
my house with the slate roof
and upstairs rooms with fireplaces.
I'm looking down on the gaslights
paling in the street: dawn, cool air,
the footsteps of the Watch.
I hear my youngest daughter
coughing up the last of illness.
My son is up, preparing the stove,
the hot water for his tea.
Soon he will go to the shop,
his work as apprentice: the fine
tools; the ridged detail of silver;
snuff boxes; plates that will be
heirlooms; memorial cups.
I lean into my wife's body,
I face the ceiling. In this life,
I sleep on the left side of the bed,
my left hand is missing a middle finger,
my two daughters have dark eyes,
my wife is a large woman
who loves music and my tenor voice.

NANA'S VISIT

She hid her bottle of port
in the kitchen washtub
and we'd catch her lifting
the porcelain lid, reaching in:
we heard a swishing, and remembered
the smell of wet newspapers
in her icebox; the hall toilet
that gargled as you froze
on the seat and strange footsteps
went past. And suddenly father
was shouting. O his mother was drunk again,
singing her old vaudeville songs,
unloosening her stiff legs.
You could almost see the music hall
lit up, the Indian clubs whirling
like a halo around her head,
up went the left leg, up the right.
We saw her steamer trunk,
the pleated panties like pink
carnations, the sharp edges
of yellow contracts, a photo
of her father, his white moustache
hung like the cliffs of Dover.
We heard the men of Tipperary
whistling would she do it again,
and she did, against the painted scenery,
the flat trees of Eden shimmering
in gaslight. Up went her skirt,
out went her bum. We heard applause,
watched her kick off her shoes
in grand finale, snuffing out
a row of candles with her naked feet.

RECONCILIATION

In darkness, like a camera, your shutter wide:
as if fathers coming upstairs could be seen,
their hands never closing the solid oak doors.
And their letters said the right thing:
"Daughter, I'm coming home. Dream of rivers."
You do. You want the exact moment
of arrival. The long water behind you
flat with dust: the sky embedded in it,
two people in a boat, their white hands
like bait in the water. You want to see him
freshly out of there: hair shaggy with weeds,
eyes like quartz, the black tunnel in his groin
filled with snails. And if he tried to speak,
you would interpret his pain to him.
You would clean him up and fit him
with a living heart. You would be
his child with the crystalline eyes.
You would step at last out of your negative.

PERSONAL

Florida woman wide-hipped pretty fair
condition mid-40s never married
seeks slender man 24–35
moderate barfly OK no politics
poor skin or Oedipists
needs loving right man open to moves
marriage likely am growing
tired of long-walk widowers
who don't smoke or swear
I sleep late lie sulk nag am bad
dreamer with mortgage paid for
central A/C who loves antique Tennyson
no Hemingways please
no Cuban spies
no hectic loners with bony fingers
used to women like clams
no fish symbolists please or
menorah saints giving orders
good talkers old-time venters
needed but I don't listen after
1 a.m. yes I'm top-heavy I've
never tried this before
good eater over 5'9" won't
go hungry hidden yard available
photo a must small feet come to me
lover of wrought iron faithful as Friday
will meet you halfway in the mail
will walk to Miami to greet you

THE WEEPER

I'm doing it openly at a Formica table
in Bickford's the waitress gives me hankies
the Puerto Rican family is waving & nodding
    my father is the counterman scraping
      his shoes poor man he steps in everything
my mother the immigrant woman mopping
the floor I weep into her bucket's milky
water O look it's never too late mother
    but the bouncer in tuxedo's coming at me

cry he says keep crying out you go you
drifter who let you in unshaven your feet
poking through sneakers sit up straight
    I see my daughter outside dancing for pennies
    I'm knocking on the window hey you hey you
my father says close your eyes we're counting
the receipts go to sleep your mother is tired
leaning on the mop O it's my sister O lucky
    brother don't stuff napkins in your mouth

quick a menu waitress where am I listen here
I am below the Saturday blue special baked
fool with hash-browns & week-old lettuce
    bring me death & pancakes bring me something
    before it's too late I can weep for at 25¢
it's my wife blowing her nose it's good she says
O lucky husband no one but you weeps so well
come to bed in the ice days of January in the
    evening beneath the quilt you can cry into my hair

Notes

"The Expulsion"

After the 15th-century painting (tempera and gold on wood), *The Creation of the World and the Expulsion from Paradise*, by Giovanni di Paolo. In other versions by di Paolo of this scene, the position of the angel's hand is not so ambiguous as he pushes Adam and Eve out of Eden.

"Refigurations"

Based on the 1989 exhibit, *Refigured Painting: The German Image 1960–88*, at the Solomon R. Guggenheim Museum in New York. Featured artists included Georg Baselitz, Jorg Immendorff, Rainer Fetting, Friedemann Hahn, Sigmar Polke, and C. O. Paeffgen, whose works provided images for this poem.

"*Les Amoureux en Vert*"

After the painting by Marc Chagall.

"Eclipse"

The epigraph is the author's translation of a passage from Paul Celan's "Psalm," from *Niemandsrose* (© 1963 by S. Fisher Verlag, Frankfurt am Main).

"Dostoevksy at Semyonov Square, 1849" (Fyodor Dostoevsky, 1821–1881)

In April 1849, members of conversation groups that met at the houses of Mikhail Petrashevsky and Sergey Durov were arrested by the Tzarist police. Their crime was that they discussed ways of changing, if not overthrowing, the Tzarist state. Around April 14, Dostoevsky had been invited to read aloud two letters to the Petrashevksy group. One letter had been written by the novelist Nikolai Gogol to the critic Visarrion Belinsky, reproving Belinsky for his review of Gogol's *Selected Passages from Correspondences with My Friends*. Belinsky, while dying of consumption, wrote a massive rejoinder of over twenty pages, viciously attacking Gogol and the Tzar's government. For reading the Belinsky letter, and for making handwritten copies of it and preparing to print it, Dostoevksy was arrested, imprisoned for eight months in the Peter and Paul Fortress, where he was interrogated, and then in December 1849 taken to Semyonov Square, at which place he heard himself condemned to death.

The evening before his arrest, Dostoevsky had been caught in a sudden rainstorm. He stopped off at the house of his friend Dr. Stephen Yanovsky to change his clothes and borrow money. Yanovsky had no money, but he did lend Dostoevsky one of his suits.

Dostoevsky's mother died in 1837, when Dostoevsky was sixteen. One of the few things he kept from her was a medallion inscribed with the motto,

> *J'ai le coeur tout plein d'amour,*
> *Quand l'aurez-vous à votre tour?*

He carried the medallion with him all his life.

A little more than two years after Dostoevsky's mother died, his father, who had been a physician at the Hospital of the Poor in Moscow, was brutally murdered by peasants.

"George Sand at Palaiseau, 1865" (George Sand, 1804–1876)

George Sand's last long-term liaison was with Alexandre Manceau, an engraver fourteen years her junior, who became her devoted secretary. After years of jealous conflict, Sand's son Maurice demanded that she choose between himself and Manceau. Sand chose Manceau, leaving the estate home at Nohant, near the town of La Châtre, to be inhabited by Maurice and his wife.

In a little country house in Palaiseau, south of Paris, Sand lived with and nursed Manceau, who was dying of tuberculosis. She had already established a relationship with the plump painter Charles Marchal, her *dernier amour*. Marie Dorval was a popular romantic actress with whom Sand probably had an affair. At the very least, they were dear friends. In her later years, Dorval could not attract much of an audience. After her death in 1849 (the year that Chopin died), her grandchildren were taken care of by Sand.

In 1830, Aurore Dupin Dudevant (George Sand's real name) reached an agreement with her philandering husband, Casimir Dudevant, that she would live part of the year in Paris away from him, and part in Nohant. In Paris, she shared a garret with her lover, the young Jules Sandeau. In collaboration with Sandeau, Aurore Dudevant wrote novelettes under the name of J. Sand. By 1832, she was writing everything herself and was known as George Sand.

"William Morris Boating up the Thames to Kelmscott Manor, 1880"
      (William Morris, 1834–96)

Morris made two trips to Iceland, in 1871 and 1873, by which time he was an established poet, designer and craftsman. In 1871, he took possession of the manor house of Kelmscott, in Oxfordshire, sharing it with his old friend, the painter and poet Dante Gabriel Rossetti (1828–1882). By this time, Rossetti and Morris's wife Jane were deeply involved with each other. By 1880, however, that relationship was effectively over, though the dying Rossetti continued to write to Jane.

"Dante's / wife jailed above the marshes of Maremma" refers to a painting by Rossetti, *La Pia de' Tolomei*, which he began in 1868 and completed in 1880. The subject of the painting is taken from the fifth canto of Dante's

Purgatorio, in which Dante is approached by the spirit of Pia de' Tolomei, who had been murdered by her husband, but first imprisoned by him in a fortress of the Maremma, a coastal region in central Italy. The portrait shows a woman impassive, resigned, while behind her, through the window of her prison, one can see the marshes (sketches of which had been supplied to Rossetti by Fairfax Murray). Next to La Pia are a breviary, a rosary, and a packet of letters written by her husband when he was her lover. The model for this painting was Jane Morris.

The source for the raw detail on the 1880 trip up the Thames is Morris's unpublished manuscript in the British Library: "Description of an expedition by boat from Kelmscott House, Upper Mall, Hammersmith, to Kelmscott Manor, Lechlade, Oxfordshire, with critical notes."

The poem deals with Morris in the period just before he became a social activist.

"Emma Goldman Deported to Russia, 1919" (Emma Goldman, 1869–1940)

Both Emma Goldman and her friend Alexander Berkman had been imprisoned in 1917 in connection with their antidraft activities. Berkman, known as "Sasha," served his time in the Federal penitentiary in Atlanta, while Goldman was incarcerated at the Federal prison in Jefferson City, Missouri, where she helped make clothing.

"Bruno Bettelheim at Dachau, 1938" (Bruno Bettelheim, 1903–1990)

Before his arrest in the spring of 1938, Dr. Bettelheim had taken an autistic child into his home. From 1938 until his release in 1939, Bettelheim was imprisoned first at Dachau, then at Buchenwald.

"Eugene O'Neill at Tao House, 1941" (Eugene O' Neill, 1888–1953)

The O'Neills had a home with Chinese motifs built in the mountains near San Francisco. It was here that O'Neill wrote *Long Day's Journey into Night*, while struggling with the familial tremor that would soon make writing physically impossible. Carlotta, his wife, had installed a player piano in "Rosie's Room," a kind of den that contained fixtures from a saloon and memorabilia of Eugene's father, the actor James O'Neill.

About the Author

Born in New York City to Helen Burghard and John K. Allman, and originally a student in science, John Allman earned a B.A. in English literature at Hunter College of the City University of New York, and an M.A. with an emphasis in creative writing at Syracuse University. His first collection of poems, *Walking Four Ways in the Wind,* appeared in the Princeton Series of Contemporary Poets, published by Princeton University Press. Three subsequent collections were published by New Directions, which also published his first book of fiction, *Descending Fire & Other Stories,* in 1994. Over the years, Allman's poems, short stories, and essays have appeared in such journals as *The Atlantic, American Poetry Review, The Antioch Review, Agni Review, Epoch, Ironwood, Massachusetts Review, The North Dakota Quarterly, Poetry, Paris Review,* and *The Quarterly.* His awards include the Helen Bullis Prize from *Poetry Northwest,* a Pushcart Prize in Poetry, and Writing Fellowships from the National Endowment for the Arts in 1984 and 1990. Poems from his collection *Scenarios for a Mixed Landscape* were used as a basis for chamber music compositions by Eric Ewazen for viola, harp, and soprano—performed for the first time at the Juilliard School in Lincoln Center on February 5, 1994. He is currently working on a novel, *The Daughters of Lazarus,* and a new collection of poems, *The Blue Gazebo.* John Allman has been teaching literature and composition at Rockland Community College since 1971. He lives in Katonah, N.Y., with his wife Eileen and has one daughter, Jennifer.

Support for this poetry series is provided by grants from Clarkson University
and The Wallace Stevens Foundation, Stamford, Connecticut.